SCIENCE & BELIEF
THE BIG ISSUES

SCIENCE & BELIEF

THE BIG ISSUES

RUSSELL STANNARD

LION

A Lion Book
an imprint of
Lion Hudson plc
Wilkinson House, Jordan Hill Road,
Oxford OX2 8DR, England
www.lionhudson.com
ISBN 978 0 7459 5572 8 (print)
ISBN 978 0 7459 5880 4 (epub)
ISBN 978 0 7459 5879 8 (Kindle)
ISBN 978 0 7459 5881 1 (pdf)

Distributed by:
UK: Marston Book Services, PO Box 269, Abingdon, Oxon, OX14 4YN
USA: Trafalgar Square Publishing, 814 N. Franklin Street, Chicago, IL 60610
USA Christian Market: Kregel Publications, PO Box 2607, Grand Rapids,
Michigan 49501

First edition 2012
10 9 8 7 6 5 4 3 2 1 0

Acknowledgments
Unless otherwise state scripture quotations are taken from the *Holy Bible,
New International Version*, copyright © 1984 International Bible Society.
Used by permission of Hodder & Stoughton, a member of the Hodder
Headline Group. All rights reserved. 'NIV' is a trademark of International
Bible Society. UK trademark number 1448790.
pp. 105, 139 Extracts from *The Authorized (King James) Version*. Rights in
the Authorized Version are vested in the Crown. Reproduced by permission of
the Crown's patentee, Cambridge University Press.

This book has been printed on paper and board independently certified
as having been produced from sustainable forests.

A catalogue record for this book is available
from the British Library

Typeset in 9.75/13 Century Schoolbook BT
Printed in Great Britain by Clays Ltd, St Ives plc

CONTENTS

INTRODUCTION

In September 2010 the main headline in *The Times* newspaper read:

'Hawking: God did not create the Universe'

The front page story began:

Just as Darwinism removed the need for a creator in the sphere of biology, Britain's most eminent scientist argues that a new series of theories have rendered redundant the role of a creator for the Universe.

At around the same time if you went into a bookshop like Waterstones, you would find prominently displayed near the entrance, among the best-sellers, Richard Dawkins's *The God Delusion*. And not just among the best-sellers, but also in the science section and the religion section; there was no escaping it. The book was a follow-up to a Channel 4 TV series of his entitled *The Root of All Evil*. No prizes for guessing what he was referring to!

Such media coverage is understandable; it sells newspapers and books and boosts viewing figures in a way that a sober title such as *God is Alive, and Still in Charge* would not. But if the media, for its own reasons, inclines towards promoting the view that science and religion are locked in conflict, it does raise the question of where you might seek the kind of information that would enable you to form a balanced and well-considered assessment of the various issues. Young people might, for example, look to school religious education (RE) lessons for guidance – at least in the UK where such lessons are part of the curriculum, unlike the situation in the USA. But to what extent are RE teachers confident about talking on scientific topics, let alone how to relate the science to religious belief? The same is likely to be true of sermons delivered in churches; to what extent are preachers equipped to speak authoritatively to their congregations on the subject?

It was thoughts like these that led me to propose that there should be a video series on the subject – one that could be used in schools and churches, and also for private study. The John Templeton Foundation generously provided the funds, and I teamed up with former BBC TV producer, Tony Coe, to create a twelve-episode series entitled *Science and Belief: The Big Issues*. Though I personally, as both a professional scientist and a licensed lay minister in the Church of England, find no conflict between science and belief, that was beside the point. The aim of the series was not to try and make converts but to present, as impartially as I could manage, the relevant background information and the arguments both for and against belief. The overall purpose was to stimulate discussion of the questions raised, and to allow each individual to make up their own mind on the issues. Tony was a great help in this respect in that he himself was a self-confessed atheist, as were several of the participants who express their views in the videos.

The series deals fairly comprehensively with the various ways in which science and belief impact on each other: Genesis and evolution, Intelligent Design, the origins of morality, the creation of the universe, the Anthropic Principle, the significance of finding extraterrestrial intelligence, insights from psychology, and the possibility of miracles.

At the time of writing, the video series and its accompanying Teachers' Notes are to be found in DVD format in 40 per cent of all UK secondary schools and in 7,500 churches. The material is also currently available for anyone to download from YouTube at http://tinyurl.com/6kkqs4n.

This book is based on that series. It allows for a more in-depth treatment of the issues. As in the video episodes, each chapter begins with a selection of the viewpoints expressed by those being interviewed. These serve to illustrate the wide range of opinions held on each subject, and give a good idea of the confusion surrounding the topic. Each chapter then ends with a set of questions – the Big Issues – for you to consider for yourself in the light of what you have read.

1 EVOLUTION AND GENESIS

- Eve being made out of Adam's rib is just a religious fairy tale.

- To say that we are all descended from Adam and Eve is daft because we would all be the same ethnicity.

- There is too much evidence in the form of fossil records to suggest that evolution has never happened or that the world was created in six days as Genesis states, but this doesn't mean that the Christian Creation story is lacking in value for me.

- At the time Genesis was written, it was a supernatural time and therefore a supernatural explanation was needed. But today we live in a scientific age and obviously we need a scientific explanation.

- A literal interpretation of Genesis is just as unrealistic as believing that there's no possibility of a God at all.

- I'm a Christian but I don't believe every word of the Bible is literally true.

Adam and Eve versus evolution. Such is the starting point for many people when trying to sort out the relationship between religious belief and modern science. And it is not difficult to see why. On the one hand we have the Genesis account of Adam being made from the dust of the ground, with God breathing into his nostrils the breath of life. As for Eve, she is made from a rib taken from Adam's side. It is all a far cry from the account given by Darwin's theory of evolution. This holds that humans evolved from more primitive ancestors. The basic idea is that in any species there are differences between its individual members. Some are faster runners than others, or have sharper claws, a thicker protective hide, better eyesight, or greater intelligence, etc. Others are less fortunate. Those lucky enough to possess a characteristic that helps them to avoid predators and find scarce food and shelter are the ones likely to live to an age where they can mate and pass on their advantageous characteristics to the next generation. Those less well endowed have a poorer chance of surviving and having offspring. Thus there is a weeding-out process whereby advantageous characteristics have a better chance of being passed on than the less advantageous ones.

In the case of cheetahs, for instance, where the characteristic we most have in mind is speed of movement, the next generation will on average be expected to be faster runners than the previous generation. And having got to the next generation, the process is all set to repeat itself, with the species becoming ever faster. And the same goes for any other characteristic conferring some sort of survival advantage. In the case of us humans: intelligence. It too will be selected out. The process happens naturally and automatically; it does not require an overseeing Intelligence to do the sorting. Moreover, it appears to be a process that would work at any level. We and the animals we see around us today have all descended from more primitive ancestors. How far does the process go back? To the inanimate chemicals lying around on the surface of the Earth when it formed 4.5 billion years ago.

The living came out of the non-living. Such is Darwin's *theory of evolution by natural selection*, as set out in his famous book *On the Origin of Species*, published in 1859. And as we have already noted, it is nothing like what we find in Genesis.

So, what are we to make of it? As a first step let me ask you where you think the following quotation comes from:

In the beginning were created only the germs or causes of the forms of life which were afterwards to be developed in gradual course.

Clearly a statement of evolution. So, a quote from Darwin, right? Actually, that was St Augustine writing in *De Genesi ad Litteram*. Augustine lived 1,500 years before Darwin.

Not that I am saying Augustine got there before Darwin – not in the sense of knowing all about the modern theory of evolution – evolution by natural selection. Of course not. But what is clear from the writings of Augustine is that he did not accept a *literal* interpretation of Genesis – the kind of interpretation some Christians put on it today. Does that make Augustine a one-off – a maverick? No. We find that most of the early church leaders did not interpret Genesis the way some fundamentalists do today – fundamentalists who, by being literal, put themselves on a collision course with science.

When it comes to reading and interpreting the Bible, the first thing to recognize is that it is not a *book*. It is a *library* of books. Books written by different authors, in different styles: history, poetry, collections of sayings, and so on. How we read a book depends on what kind of writing it is supposed to be. Choose a book from an ordinary library and open it at random...

Tyger! Tyger! burning bright
In the forests of the night...

No one in their right mind will read this as a literal account of what actually happened. A tiger on fire?! It is immediately obvious that this piece of literature is an example of poetry. Poets are allowed to say such things. And for good reason. When William Blake goes on to speak of "the fire in the eyes", he is endeavouring to convey the intensity of the look on the face of the tiger. He is re-creating in the reader something of the same emotional response you would have if confronted in a forest by a fierce tiger.

A purely *scientific* account would point out that there was in fact no burning, no rise in temperature. The diameter of the pupils of the tiger's eyes had dilated by a certain number of millimetres. But that was all. So what does that mean? The author, William Blake, has been caught out by science? Of course not. Poetry has its own way of getting at certain kinds of truth. And this proves to be more effective than a purely factual, cold recitation of what is actually happening physically. For this reason we willingly surrender ourselves to the convention of accepting the poet's approach to matters. We do this in much the same way as a devotee of opera, or Andrew Lloyd Webber musicals, is prepared to suspend disbelief at the absurdity of people bursting out into song rather than just talking to each other, in order to be swept along on a deeply felt tide of emotion – an experience hard to create in any other way.

So it is that we have to ask ourselves what kind of writing we are confronted with when opening the Bible. It all depends on where exactly we open it. There are certainly parts of it that are intended as a historical record of something that actually did happen: the teachings of Jesus, the accounts of his crucifixion and resurrection, and so on. Even here, however, we have to be careful. Just because we might classify some passage in the Bible as a "historical account" does not necessarily mean that it was written in the style that a modern historian would adopt. Modern historians attempt to give accurate and authoritative accounts of what actually happened. Their intention is to be objective. Admittedly this might not be easy. Their own personal views are liable to colour their interpretation. British and Argentinian historians are liable to put a different gloss on their accounts of the Falklands War, for instance. But regardless of how successful or not they might be in avoiding such pitfalls, the intention is clear: they try to present a sober, impartial record of the events as they actually happened.

Not so the early Jewish historians. Their prime intention was to show God working out his purpose over time. History and theology became inextricably mixed up. Their writings were meant to inspire and uplift. One of the aims was to hold up to the youth of the nation fine examples of ancestors they could model themselves on. It became common practice for notable deeds carried out by descendants to be transposed in time and accorded to the venerated founder of the tribe. In this way victories were won posthumously! Then there was the question of a person's age. Unlike the situation today where older people are treated with scant respect ("on the scrap heap at forty"), in those times great age was synonymous with being wise. The older you were, the more experience you must have had, and the more valuable your advice. In the cause of honouring the great figures of the past, how better than to add a few years to their age – then a few more for luck: Moses 120 years old, Isaac 180 years. Effectively this is saying that in order to be as wise as these great leaders, you would expect that you would normally have had to live to such an age.

With such cautionary thoughts in mind, we have to ask what kind of writing we face when we open it at the book of Genesis. Here we must be guided by biblical scholars. The majority of them describe the writing here as an example of *myth*. To avoid misunderstanding let me say straightaway that words have a habit of changing their meaning over time. The word "gay" is a modern example of how dramatically a word can acquire a meaning it did not earlier have. The same has been true of the word "myth". Today, in normal conversation, if I call something a myth, I am dismissing it as something that is not true. But in the context of biblical study, it refers to an ancient narration which, fair enough, describes something that did not actually happen – not as such – that was not the point. No, it was a narration for addressing deep timeless questions about existence and purpose. It was the kind of story by which ancient civilizations – not just the Jews, but *all* ancient civilizations – passed on from one generation to the next the fruits of their wisdom – the conclusions they had drawn from experience.

What kinds of conclusions? Well, to begin with, the Genesis creation story tells us that we were made by God. We owe everything to God – our very existence. As a consequence, we owe him our loyalty. Our lives are not our own to do with as we please. They are a gift from God, and we should live them the way God intends that we should live them.

Not that this is easy. From the moment of conception, we have a built-in tendency to be self-centred rather than God-centred. This tendency is sometimes referred to as *original sin*. It derives from that part of the Genesis story to do with the taking of the forbidden fruit. Adam and Eve were disobedient. They wanted to have things their way rather than follow God's instructions. For this transgression they, and their descendants (you and me), were banished from Paradise. No matter how hard we try to build a paradise here on Earth we are doomed to fail because of this self-centred streak in each and every one of us.

Not that all is gloom and doom. The creation story goes on to say how we were made in the image of God. One way of understanding this is to say that, despite our fallen nature, we have the potential to be Godlike. Thus Genesis sets the scene for life's drama. We start our lives centred on ourselves with our own needs and desires foremost in our minds. But the aim of life is to change our mind (that is to say "repent") and re-centre our lives on God.

Then there are other messages in that story. Eve being made from a rib taken from Adam's side. It is highly unlikely that this was ever intended as a literal account of how women originated. Rather, it is saying that man is not complete without woman and woman is not complete without man. It is drawing attention to the importance of marriage. It is holding up the ideal that a man and woman in marriage should be so committed to each other as to become "one flesh".

Finally there is the idea that Adam and Eve were not put into the Garden of Eden to laze about and have a good time. They were put there to till the soil and look after the garden. Might that not be regarded as an early version of the modern-day Green Message – the notion that we humans are not here on planet Earth to exploit it, but to look after it in a responsible manner?

Such then are the types of truth the ancient Jewish people wished to pass on to future generations, and they did it in story form. Why story form? Why not set it down in plain language? Here we have to recall that in those times most people could neither read nor write. They had to remember what was told to them aurally. And people are just not very good at remembering what they have been told. Though it does have to be said, ancient people were much better at it than we are today. We like to write things down and look things up in books and on the Internet. That was not an option back then. They had to practise learning things off by heart. We, in contrast, tend today to discount learning things by rote. The ancients came to recognize that there was one form of narration that was much easier to remember than any other, and that was a story. You recall how the story begins. That in turn jogs the memory of what happened next. Which in turn prompts the memory of what happened after that. And before you know it, you have remembered the whole story line. Thus the ancients took a story – one vivid in its imagery – and grafted onto it the timeless truths they wished to pass on.

This storytelling was still prevalent at the time of Jesus. He taught through parables. Storytelling was ingrained in the culture in such a way that he was able to plunge straight into it without any prefatory remarks making it clear that what was to follow was just a story. The parable of the Good Samaritan, for example, does not begin "I want you to imagine that there was a man on the road from Jerusalem to Jericho. Let's say he was set upon by thieves…" No, Jesus just goes straight in with an attention-grabbing, direct kind of prose that makes it *sound* as though the incident actually happened as described. Jesus could do this, confident that his hearers all subscribed willingly to the common storytelling culture. Such a way of speaking was taken for granted.

We can see something of this same kind of tradition lingering on in our own times. You have only to think of William Golding's *The Lord of the Flies*, or George Orwell's *Animal Farm*. Both are fictional stories, but they convey disturbing truths about ourselves. Indeed, to a lesser extent, TV soaps can sometimes cause us to think about our own situation in life and how we might meet its challenges.

But generally speaking, we live today in a culture that tends to tell things the way they are. We prefer a more scientific, pragmatic approach. And there is much to be said for this. Except, of course, when it comes to reading texts written according to a quite different convention – like that of Genesis.

We are faced then with a situation where, broadly speaking, we can regard Genesis as dealing with a different set of questions to those addressed by science. This is often described as the difference between how-type questions and why-type questions. Whereas science is concerned with the mechanics of *how* we humans developed from more primitive ancestors, religion is more concerned with what the ultimate purpose of life might be: *why* are we here?

If this is the case, why do so many people today insist on adopting a literal approach to Genesis – one that inevitably puts them on a collision course with science? Why do some go as far as to try and have the Adam and Eve account taught in school science lessons as a rival theory to that of evolution? They doubtless do this out of a deep reverence for the Bible, and in the belief that they are defending the original way in which the account was meant to be read. But, as we have seen, early church leaders, way back in the fourth century, did not see Genesis in that light.

Some scholars claim that the ascendancy of the literal interpretation of Genesis did not really happen until the sixteenth century – the time of the Reformation. This was when Protestants were breaking away from the rule of Rome. It was a drastic course of action. What was their justification for doing this? What was their authority? The Bible. The Bible was to be their authority, not the Pope any longer.

Those remaining loyal to Rome protested that, while continuing to accept the authority of the Pope, they too revered the Bible. The two sides vied with each other over which of them respected the Bible more, to the extent that at the Council of Trent, held in the 1540s to define the Roman church's stance in the face of the defection, a decree was issued that God himself was the author of the Bible. The Bible had been written "at the dictation of the Holy Spirit". The Old Testament writers, along with Matthew, Mark, Luke, and John – all they had been doing was taking down dictation. The Bible was the inerrant word of God.

This understanding of the Bible always had its problems. It was hard to account for the markedly different styles of writing as you went from one book to another. Even more disturbing were the inconsistencies that became apparent when comparing one part of the Bible with another. For example, we have been talking of "the creation story". But there are two of them. One begins at the start of chapter 1 of Genesis, and the second begins at verse 4 of chapter 2. They contradict each other. So what are we to conclude? God, when writing Genesis, had forgotten how he made the world? Or take Jesus' resurrection appearances. According to Matthew and Mark, the disciples had to go to Galilee in order to see the risen Christ. But Luke has it that they met in Jerusalem, while John has them meeting him in both locations. Another memory lapse by the infallible God?!

The situation was not remedied until 1962 at another council – Vatican II. This gave rise to two authoritative documents. One of them, *Dei Verbum* (or *Word of God*), was intended to spell out the church's understanding of the nature of revelation; that is, the process whereby God communicates with human beings. There it spoke of Scripture as being written at the *inspiration* of the Holy Spirit. *Inspiration* not dictation. It went on:

> *Since God speaks in Sacred Scripture through men in human*
> *fashion, the interpreter of Sacred Scripture, in order to see*
> *clearly what God wanted to communicate to us, should carefully*
> *investigate what meaning the sacred writers really intended,*
> *and what God wanted to manifest by means of their words.*

It was a statement that recognized that the writers had their own purposes in writing; the words were their own, and not necessarily God's.

**Which of the following statements,
in your opinion, gives the better
assessment of the relationship between
evolution and Genesis?**

They are in conflict with each other.

**They are seeking different kinds
of truth.**

2 INTELLIGENT DESIGN

- Evolution clearly shows that we are descended from apes.

- The body is so intricate that it must have a designer and that designer must be God.

- At various places in the evolutionary process there's big steps that couldn't have come on its own, such as the creation of the first cell or the creation of the eye. I think that's where God steps in to help the process.

- Evolution has taken over 3 billion years, so of course there's plenty of time to get from primordial mud to us without the need to involve a God.

- I accept evolution, though I also believe in God. I think that evolution is a logical process, but I also believe that it was God's way of kick starting everything.

- I believe that evolution was God's way of creating all life forms and how we end up in God's plan.

- God couldn't have used evolution to make mankind in his own image because evolution uses random chance and therefore he had no way of knowing what he'd end up with.

– Darwin makes you feel really depressed. We
 want to think we're special. If we're not special,
 what's the point?

You are out for a walk on the beach when, lying among the
pebbles, you see a watch. Even if you were an alien from
another planet and had never seen a watch before, you would
immediately recognize that this was something that could not
have been fashioned by natural forces – the way the pebbles,
through centuries of pounding by the sea, had developed their
similar rounded appearance. The mechanism of the watch is just
too complicated and intricate. It shows all the signs of having
been designed to fulfil a function.

In the same way, it can be argued that everything about the
human body is so beautifully fitted to fulfil its function (with
the possible exception of the appendix) that the whole ensemble
must have been designed – and the designer must be God. Such
was the line of reasoning put forward by the theologian William
Paley in 1802. The need for a Divine Watchmaker was deemed to
be a proof of the existence of God.

But then, as we have seen, along came Charles Darwin with
his theory of evolution by natural selection – a process whereby
humans, and all the other animals we see today, could have
evolved from very primitive beginnings by purely natural means
not requiring the intervention of any conscious designer.

There is considerable misunderstanding over evolution. Time
and again we hear the argument that blind chance alone could
not conceivably have given rise to such intricate organisms.
Chance certainly has a part to play. Offspring resemble their
parents because they share the same genetic material. This is
in the form of a long helically shaped molecule called the *DNA
molecule*. It is made up from a chain of smaller molecular units.
The order in which these smaller units appear along the chain
constitutes, in effect, a code. This code governs your physical

characteristics – your species, colour of eyes, height, intelligence, instinctive behaviour, etc. The DNA of the offspring originates as copies of the DNA of the parents. In the copying process, random mistakes sometimes occur. This gives rise to new variations of coding corresponding to variations in physical characteristics. It is these novel characteristics so produced upon which the principle of natural selection gets to work. But it is a mistake to think that what is going on is purely down to blind chance. Whereas the bringing about of mutations certainly involves randomness, there is also the systematic weeding out of the inferior characteristics – the process of natural selection – and this is anything but random.

As an analogy think of hens laying eggs. The eggs are of various sizes – a random process. The battery farmer wishes to separate out the larger eggs to sell at a premium price. This he can do by deliberately and painstakingly sorting out the eggs by hand. Alternatively, the eggs can be directed onto a sieve with holes such that the medium-sized eggs (there never seem to be eggs designated "small") pass through leaving the larger ones – a physical selection process requiring no conscious thought on the part of the farmer, but achieving exactly the same end. That is how it is with evolution by natural selection.

What is the evidence for it? First, we have the fossil record. Generally speaking, the earlier fossils, as expected, are to be found in the lower strata of rock, these having been laid down before the upper ones. We say "generally" because the Earth's crust moves and in some places there is uplift and distortion of the layers. But the overall pattern is clear and allows us to trace how the species developed over time from more primitive forms to what we find today.

But there are gaps in the fossil record. This is an objection often raised against the theory. However, this is only to be expected. In the first place some species do not leave fossil traces. Then you have to take note that, because of the movements of the Earth's crust, some fossils are expected to be lost through subduction – one tectonic plate passing under another, carrying its embedded fossils with it. In any case, the tendency is for many of the gaps to be closed as more and more finds are made.

A second line of evidence in favour of evolution comes from anatomical comparisons that can be made between species. And yet another comes from DNA comparisons. The latter provides a powerful, quantitative measure of how closely two species are related. For instance, we humans share between 96 and 99 per cent of our genetic material with chimpanzees, depending on how exactly we wish to make the comparison. The similarity between us and mice is roughly 92 per cent, a fruit fly 44 per cent, yeast 26 per cent, a weed 18 per cent, and so on.

Finally we mention the fact that we can observe evolution going on in our own time. An often cited example concerns moths that began by being light in colour, but with succeeding generations gradually became darker. These changes coincided with the onset of the industrial revolution and the way in which the buildings upon which the moths habitually alighted became dirtier as a result of the sooty atmosphere. Those moths that happened by chance to be slightly darker in colour tended to escape the notice of predators; they were to some extent camouflaged. These were the ones that survived to the point where they could have offspring inheriting their darker markings. In this way the members of the species living in industrial areas progressively became darker. On the passing of clean air legislation and the subsequent cleaning of buildings, this evolutionary process was halted and indeed to some extent reversed! The manner in which insects and other pests gradually develop immunity to the pesticides meant to control them is another example of evolution in action today.

The theory of evolution holds that not only did we humans develop out of the same ancestors as the apes, but the process goes right back to the inanimate chemicals that lay on the surface of the Earth after its formation – what is sometimes called the *primordial mud,* or primordial slime. In other words, life developed out of the non-living. For the biologist, something is held to be "living" if it satisfies a certain set of criteria. There are various ways of expressing this but the list usually includes such characteristics as *nutrition*: the ability to take in substances from the environment and use them to promote growth and provide energy for the body's activities; *growth*: with changes in shape as well as size; *respiration*: the process of breaking down substances to release energy; *reproduction*: by either sexual or asexual means; *excretion*: the capacity to get rid of unwanted substances; and *responsiveness*: the characteristic of responding to one's environment. Inanimate objects might possess one or more of these properties. A crystal can grow; a nail can respond to the environment by becoming rusty. But to be classed as "living", the combination is needed. And that is all. There is no special ingredient called "life" that has to be added to what is going on physically.

The overwhelming majority of scientists go along with evolution. So why do some people have reservations about it? Well, it surely does seem to be a gigantic leap to go from inanimate chemicals to you and me. There appear to have been some steps along the way that must have been exceptionally difficult to negotiate in any natural way: the formation of the first cell, the formation of the first multicellular organism, the ear, the eye, and so on. Many religious believers claim that these steps could not have been bridged in any natural way. While accepting that evolution might have taken place, this was to only a limited degree. It required the direct, active intervention of God to overcome these hurdles. This viewpoint is known as *Intelligent Design*, or ID. It is a viewpoint particularly prevalent in the USA.

Darwin himself was fully aware of the difficulties posed to his theory by these seemingly big steps in the evolutionary chain. In *On the Origin of Species,* he wrote:

To suppose that the eye with all its inimitable contrivances
for adjusting the focus to different distances, for admitting
different amounts of light, and for the correction of spherical
and chromatic aberration, could have been formed by
natural selection, seems, I freely confess, absurd in the
highest degree...

And yet he was to go on later in the book to affirm that this could have been achieved in a succession of small changes, progressively building up to the final product, provided that each of these changes conferred on the individual some survival value, however marginal. Only so could the advantage be preserved ready for the next move to be added.

One possible scenario for the development of the eye is to begin very simply with the appearance of a small patch of skin that was particularly sensitive to light – the first rudiments of a retina. It would allow for the detection of a shadow – one that might indicate the presence of a predator, and hence be the signal to take prompt avoiding action. Next, the sensitive skin patch might find itself in a gradually developing hollow. This would confer a further advantage in that, depending on which side of the patch registered the shadow, one would have an indication of the direction in which the supposed predator might lie. This in turn would act as a guide as to the direction in which it would be prudent to flee – something previously unknown. But, of course, the trouble with hollows is that they tend to collect dirt. This could be countered if a transparent jelly-like substance were to accumulate in the hollow. This would keep the dirt out while permitting the light still to get to the putative retina. Furthermore, were that jelly-like substance to subsequently develop a bulge, that would in effect constitute a lens. Now one is registering not a crude, ambiguous shadow but an image – one that would allow the determination of whether one was indeed dealing with a predator to be avoided, or more hopefully with prey that could be hunted as the source of one's next meal. A variable-sized opening (or pupil) to deal with different light intensities would be a further refinement, as too would be adjustable shutters (eyelids) for added protection of the delicate lens, and the ability to produce water (tear ducts) to clean the lens.

All this, of course, is pure guesswork. There is no way of establishing for certain that this suggested scenario was in fact followed. We were not around to witness it. But no matter. What has been demonstrated is that there is at least one possible route by which the complexity of the eye might have arisen through a succession of small, reasonably plausible changes, each of which confers a measure of benefit to the recipient and so would have been preserved ready for further elaboration later.

But, it will be argued, won't such a process, involving as it does so many tiny incremental changes over successive generations, take for ever to accomplish? This is where we have to take note of another scientific advance: the recognition of the amount of time that has been available since the Earth formed. One recalls how, in the seventeenth century, Bishop Ussher wrote an article entitled "A Chronological Index of the Years and Times from Adam unto Christ, Proved by Scripture", in which he famously undertook to calculate the age of the Earth by adding together the ages of all the relevant Old Testament characters, each at the time they begat the next in line. He arrived at the conclusion:

Whereupon we reckon that from Adam unto Christ are three thousand, nine hundred and seventy four years, six months and ten days.

I love the "ten days" bit! So, adding on the 2,000 years that have elapsed since Christ, we would conclude that the world came into existence some 6,000 years ago.

In contrast, modern-day geologists, using radioactive dating techniques, put the age of the Earth at 4.5 *billion* years! This conclusion receives backing from astronomers. Their observations show that the big bang origins of the universe happened 13.7 billion years ago. You would expect the Earth to have formed sometime after the universe as a whole came into existence. So the two figures are consistent. And they are nothing like what you might conclude from a literal interpretation of Scripture.

Billions of years. Our minds simply cannot envisage such enormous spans of time. Suffice to say, evolutionary biologists are convinced that no matter how drawn out the process might be with its succession of incremental changes, there has been plenty of time available for evolution, without direct divine aid, to take us from primordial mud to where we are today.

Having said all that, there are, nevertheless, those who remain unconvinced and continue to subscribe to Intelligent Design. The danger of doing so is that ID is essentially a "God of the gaps" type of argument. By that is meant that one points to something scientists cannot explain (or at least have not *yet* explained) and says in effect, "Scientists cannot explain that. Why? Because God is doing that." The trouble with that line of reasoning is that the gaps have a nasty habit of getting filled up, leaving such an intervening type of God with less and less to do. Thunder and lightning was a classic example of this. These were long regarded as manifestations of God venting his wrath. That was before Benjamin Franklin flew his kite in a thunderstorm and demonstrated that it was merely an electrical phenomenon. As an aside, I should perhaps add that although some believers might have regretted the loss of this so-called evidence for God's existence, others warmly welcomed the discovery. It had for a long time been a mystery as to why the church spires built to the glory of God had so consistently been the objects of his wrath. Before the subsequent invention of the lightning rod, it is on record that no fewer than 103 bell ringers had been killed by lightning strikes between 1753 and 1786 in France alone!

So, given the evidence for evolution, how do we summarize the options open to the religious believer? We saw in the previous chapter how those who continue to adhere to a literal interpretation of the Genesis account of Adam and Eve inevitably put themselves on a collision course with science. ID is at least a step on the way towards acknowledging that evolution has taken place. But does it go far enough?

A third approach for the believer is the wholesale acceptance that evolution alone got us all the way from primordial mud to where we are today. All this was done according to natural processes. Evolution was God's chosen method of creating us humans and all other living creatures. Two arguments have been advanced against this conclusion.

In the first place, it has been pointed out that evolution is based on chance: random mutations to the DNA coding. Start evolution all over again, on another planet, say, and you would have no idea what you were going to end up with. If God's aim was to produce humans who could enter into a meaningful relationship with him, why would he embark on such a haphazard, unpredictable course of action?

In this connection, one should perhaps begin by pointing out that the type of God Christians traditionally believe in is claimed to have foreknowledge. The future is already known to God. But quite apart from that, there is from biology itself an answer to this objection. It has comparatively recently come to light that it is simply not true to say that the random chance that lies at the basis of the evolutionary process makes the outcome wholly unpredictable. We have seen that the randomness is tempered by the systematic selection procedure. This ensures that characteristics conducive to survival will emerge. These characteristics include, for example, the ability to see. There is great survival value in being able to see, and we note that this ability has developed in several different ways. There is the camera-like eye of us humans and many other animals, but also the compound eye of the fly. This developed independently. It is an alternative means of achieving the same end. Start evolution all over again somewhere else, and you can be pretty sure creatures, one way or another, will develop the ability to use light as an aid to survival; they will be able to see. The same goes for the use of sound – the ability to hear. And most important of all, there will develop creatures that are intelligent. Thus evolution is not such a hit-and-miss procedure as was once thought.

The situation is similar to what happens at a horse race. At the start, we cannot be sure who will be the winner. And yet, despite the uncertainties, one outcome is more or less assured: by the end of the day, the bookmaker will have made a profit. Evolution is a bit like that. Yes, there are uncertainties. We are not able to predict exactly what the result will be. But various *general* features almost inevitably will arise. This emergence of common characteristics is called *convergence*. So, having set aside the Divine Watchmaker, perhaps we should embrace the Divine Bookmaker model!

As for the second objection to regarding evolution as God's chosen method of making us, this is based on all the suffering that goes on in the animal kingdom. It is integral to the evolutionary process that animals with the less advantageous characteristics are eliminated before they get the chance to mate and pass on their inferior genes to the next generation. The premature death of many animals, by starvation, disease, or the violent action of predators, is an essential feature of the process. This naturally raises the problem of why a supposedly good and loving God would employ such a cruel method for bringing us into existence. It is a powerful objection, and those making it deserve some kind of response.

At the outset, we perhaps need to take note of the extent to which suffering depends on the state of the mind – what it is focused upon at the time. A footballer, for instance, at the conclusion of a game might be surprised to find a graze on his knee. He cannot recall sustaining the injury; he was too preoccupied at the time in getting the ball. Under different circumstances – attending the doctor's surgery to receive an injection, say – his reaction might be altogether different. The discomfort of the needle prick is magnified out of all proportion because he is anticipating the sensation of pain; his attention is focused on the action.

This leads one to speculate that animals, with their less developed brains, might have less mental capacity to focus on the pain caused by injury, and as a result experience a lower degree of pain. We ourselves have no way of gauging the pain experienced by others. It could be that the problem of pain is not as great for animals as it is for humans. But what if this is wishful thinking? We know that there is a widespread tendency, particularly for pet owners, to assume unthinkingly that animals experience and feel things the way we humans do. This is known as anthropomorphism.

But what if they do feel pain as intensely as they appear to do? How can we come to terms with a supposedly loving God who allows this to happen? It is at this point we have to face up to the question as to what alternative approach was open to God. The aim was to bring into existence living creatures that could relate to God and respond to him in love. So, does he sit down at his drawing board to draw up the specification? In this scenario, he would then construct us, atom by atom, according to the blueprint. When it comes to our brain, he would piece it together in much the same way as an electronic engineer assembles the chips that make up a computer. And, having completed the hardware, he would then install the software.

Had God adopted this approach, and the final product went on to declare, "I love you, God. I wish to devote my life to you," would God have felt he had satisfactorily accomplished his purpose? Most unlikely. The declaration would be nothing more than an automatic output from the programming. Such a consciously assembled set of components would result in the production of a robot, not a human being who could experience genuine, spontaneous love.

For love to be real, it has to be freely offered. There has to be the risk that it will not be so offered. Love has to be won. It has to be given voluntarily; it cannot be forced or coerced. A genuine bond of love can be established only between those who start out being independent of each other. There has to be a coming together – a surrender of our isolation. But how can that be achieved between God and humans, given that the humans are entirely dependent for their very existence on God? It is not as though there were several creator gods, and a human made by one god was won over by another god. This is the dilemma that faced God: given that he was the sole creator, how to endow his creatures with a measure of independence from him in order that he might genuinely win them over. His answer? Chance. God would *not* specify all the details of our construction. He set in motion the broad principles of evolution and then let nature take its course. In a sense, we made ourselves.

And, yes, this process did involve pain, suffering, unfairness, and death. These afflicted not only the animals caught up in the evolutionary chain leading to ourselves, but are a common feature of everyday life for us humans now. God raising love to be the highest good could offer no guarantee against such eventualities. Indeed there seems to be an indissoluble link between love and suffering; you cannot have one without the other; they are opposite sides of the same coin. Proof of love does not come from having good times together, partying, having fun, enjoying an easy comfortable life, engaging in sex, and so on. Though these might indeed feature in a loving relationship, they do not constitute *proof* of love. Such activities and experiences are enjoyable in themselves. No, if we are seeking *proof* of love, then we must look to times of hardship, deprivation, and suffering. It comes from the way one is prepared to put oneself out for the other, sacrificing one's own interests for the sake of the beloved.

We see this in the example set by God himself. How do we *know* God loves us? It is because God himself suffered for us through the cruel death of his Son on the cross. It would have been all too easy for God merely to offer us comfort and encouragement from the sidelines as we had to contend with our troubles alone. But this he did not do. He allowed himself to share in our suffering. There was no other way for him to confirm the nature of his relationship with us. And if God himself, and we humans, have to suffer, then it should not be surprising that the animals have to do so too.

And as for the unfairness of animals with the less well-endowed genes having to experience premature death, we find the same kind of question raised in the context of the premature death of human infants. Such early deaths have always posed a problem for believers. It has had to be a matter of faith that God, through a life beyond death, can make good the apparent inequalities of our earthly lives. In the end all will be well. This, of course, is no answer to the basic unfairness of the evolutionary process. All I am saying is that acceptance of evolutionary theory does not pose any fresh challenge. The deep mystery of premature death, and indeed the other manifestations of life being unfair, has always been with us.

Talk about life beyond death brings us to one final question posed to religious believers by evolutionary theory. Traditionally it is held that we humans have an immortal spirit; we shall continue to exist, in some form or other, beyond death. Animals have no such spirit. Parents have to break the news to their children that their pet cats and dogs will not be accompanying them to heaven. But, given that we are ourselves evolved animals, how can such a clear-cut distinction still be made?

Some believers might respond that although we have now to come to terms with the fact that it is no longer defensible to hold that there is a *qualitative* difference between us and the other animals, we are so much further advanced intellectually than them that there is a *quantitative* difference so marked that, to all intents and purposes, we are unique in having this spiritual capacity. That might well be the case. But it still leaves the question as to how we acquired this unique spiritual capacity. Was there some point along the evolutionary chain when God said in effect, "Right. That's good enough. Let's pop the spirit in now"? Not very likely. Perhaps a more plausible idea would be that, in parallel with the evolution of our bodies, there was a gradual, progressive evolution of the spirit. What is meant by that? Presumably somewhere along the line, one of our early ancestors was the first to wonder whether there might be more to life than eating, drinking, and having sex. Was there a purpose to life? Where did everything come from? Is there anything beyond this life? As soon as this happened, there opened up the possibility of some form of communication with God – a relationship with God. For the first time in history it began to make sense to think of there being a spiritual dimension to life. That ancestor could be thought to have acquired a primitive form of spirit. By that I mean that in a life beyond death there could be a dim awareness of what was going on. Not the rich kind of relationship with God some fully evolved humans might attain, but nevertheless something worthwhile. Then with succeeding generations, especially those that followed on from the invention of speech and the mutual enrichment of thoughts and insights that such enhanced communication was able to bring about, the spiritual experience became deeper, until we reached the capacity we have today.

This is, of course, mere speculation. And yet, much like our earlier speculation as to how the eye might have developed, it is important to establish that acceptance of evolutionary theory does not necessarily lead to a contradiction with what we find to be the situation today. There needs to be at least a plausible scenario by which we might account for how the present state of affairs could have arisen. A gradual evolution of the spirit seems to provide such a scenario.

Is evolution on its own able to account for the development of intelligent life?

If so, does that get rid of God, or might we see God working through evolution?

3 MORALITY

- Our sense of morality comes from God.

- I don't think that morality can be said to come directly from religion. I don't believe that prior to the Ten Commandments people were going around killing and raping and stealing.

- Morality comes from society and our parents and it's ridiculous to say that if you're not religious then you can't be moral.

- Evolution is all about survival of the fittest. Therefore I think genetically influenced behavioural patterns lead us to being naturally selfish.

- The want to help others and the selfless need to do so is an innate ability that was given by God.

- I think the sole reason that humans behave altruistically is because it's an evolutionary advantage.

- I think that science has nothing to do with morality. If it wasn't given morality from religion then humanity would have no limits.

- Well, I do think there's a huge difference between the religious purpose and the socially constructed purpose that many people choose

to follow their lives by, but that's not to say the
two can't coexist.

– In an increasingly secular society it will be
interesting to see if morality continues.

It is wrong to steal or to commit murder. It is good to give to
charities helping the starving peoples overseas. Such statements
command almost universal acceptance. But why? What is the
source of morality?

Religious believers hold that the moral sense comes from God.
We owe our lives – our very existence – to God. That being so,
we should live our lives as God intended. We are not to use our
possessions in any way we please. They are gifts from God and,
as good stewards, we have been entrusted to use them according
to God's wishes. How are we to find out what those wishes might
be? We have been given the Ten Commandments. We have
the teachings and examples of Moses and the other prophets,
of Jesus, the saints, and other great religious leaders such as
Muhammad.

What of those who do not subscribe to any religion? It perhaps
needs to be said at the outset that such people are right to be
indignant at any suggestion that, just because they are not
religious, they cannot be moral. Though it might be true that
those of a religious persuasion might tend, *on average,* to be
better behaved than those without religious scruples, we all know
examples of people of exemplary character who are irreligious.
Where do such people get their moral sense from?

The claim is that morality stems from society; it is *we* who decide
what it shall be. And the fact that there are often disputes as to
what is, and is not, permissible provides strong support for that
viewpoint. We have only to think of such issues as abortion, the
use of embryos in stem cell research, sex before marriage, genetic
engineering, dietary prohibitions, arguments over whether there

is such a thing as a just war, and so on. Over issues such as these, well-intentioned people can arrive at diametrically opposed views. This serves to demonstrate that either God has given us guidance but there is yet plenty of room for interpretation, or alternatively morality is just a social convention.

If it is the latter, then we have still to ask on what basis a religion-less society might reach its conclusions as to what constitutes good behaviour and should be encouraged, and what is bad and should be condemned. Are there certain principles that are so manifestly "a good thing" that they inevitably command universal acceptance?

As a test case, take the example of a Nazi SS officer involved in the Holocaust. What he did is universally condemned as being wrong. But why? What might be the overarching principle he violated? How would we convince *him* that what he was doing was wrong?

We might seek to change his mind by saying that it is always wrong to kill another person. Except we have already noted there is no universal agreement that this rule is valid for all situations (abortion, just wars, mercy killing, etc).

How about a desire to bring about a better world? Surely we cannot argue with that. The SS officer agrees, but is genuinely convinced that the world would be a better place without Jews. As far as he is concerned, his engagement in the Holocaust was a means of "cleansing" the world.

Yet another alternative might be the dictum that you should do to others as you would have them do to you. The SS officer would not have wanted to change places with his victims, so that surely would convince him that what he was doing was wrong. Or would it? The officer could argue that it was impossible for him to imagine himself in the place of the Jewish victims because he was not himself Jewish. Being Jewish was what the Holocaust was all about. Given his mindset regarding Jews, he might even go as far as to convince himself that if by any chance it had turned out that he was himself a Jew, he would have been content for his fellow officers to send him to the gas chamber because the world would have been a better place without him and his like.

All this serves to illustrate how difficult it might be to set up a universally accepted secular code of morality – one that does not appeal to a higher authority, such as God. A further difficulty is that society is, and always has been, permeated throughout by religion. It is woven inextricably into the culture. Even without receiving an overtly religious upbringing, it is hard, if not impossible, for us to avoid absorbing some of the traditional religious values and outlook. For instance, the principle cited above of doing to others as you would have them do to you is just another version of "love your neighbour as yourself" – one of the teachings of Jesus. Whether a strictly secular society would have arrived at such a set of values in the absence of a religious input is impossible to tell.

So, where does that leave us? Does science have anything to say on the subject? Our first instinct is to respond: No. Time and again it is held that science is "value free". It tells us how things *are*, but cannot tell us how things *ought* to be. To a large extent this is undoubtedly true. But is that the last word? Has science nothing to say on the subject?

When we examine the behaviour of animals, we discover that much of it is *genetically determined*. By that we mean there is written into the animal's genes (i.e. DNA) a code. This code inclines the animal, when confronted with a particular set of circumstances, to respond automatically – without thinking. Your pet cat, for instance, sees a bird. It pounces, plays with it, then kills it. Why? Why do such a cruel thing? In order to have a meal? Sometimes, maybe. But what of those occasions when it is full to bursting with the cat food kindly provided by yourself? It still behaves in the same fashion, even though there appears to be no need. The trouble is that it cannot help itself. It is programmed to do that. In the distant past, the cat's ancestors were faced with a shortage of food. Those quickest off the mark were the ones most likely to catch their prey and survive. There was survival value in having an innate tendency to react automatically to the sight of a bird rather than having to think things out from scratch each time, by which time the bird had flown away. And that is how today's domesticated cat comes to have that instruction written into *its* DNA, even though today there is no longer any need for it. We say its behaviour is genetically determined.

Now, if we see that going on in animals, then we, as an evolved animal ourselves, must expect something of the same sort of thing to be going on in us. That is not to say that our behaviour is genetically *determined* – that we are helpless to do anything but blindly follow what our genes tell us to do – like some robot. No. We are self-conscious. We have the ability to reflect on and consider various options open to us. If we so decide, we can go against the genetic tendency. Nevertheless, our behaviour is almost certainly genetically *influenced*. We have an inborn tendency to behave in certain ways. It takes a conscious effort to act otherwise. Which raises the obvious question: In what ways are we inclined to behave?

As we have seen, evolution is about surviving to the point where we can mate and pass on our genes to the next generation. If there is a shortage of food, there is obvious advantage in grabbing for oneself whatever is going. So we would expect that those with a natural tendency to be selfish – disregarding the needs of others – would be the ones more likely to survive and, in so doing, pass on the genetic tendency to be selfish. Indeed, there could be further advantage in being overtly aggressive should the need arise. We do not need to look too deeply into human behaviour to see examples of those traits at work in even the youngest infants.

Our inherent self-centredness, manifest from childhood, has long been recognized. It is there in the Adam and Eve story – the episode of the taking of the forbidden fruit. Adam and Eve had all they could have possibly needed. There was just this one tree that was not theirs and they had to leave alone. But they did not; they were disobedient. They took that which was not theirs. For this reason they were banned from Paradise – they and their descendants. From the moment of conception we are inclined to be disobedient to God; we have this character flaw; we are self-centred rather than God-centred. As we noted previously, it is what theologians call "original sin". Thus Genesis sets the scene for all that is to follow: namely our need to repent and, by an act of the conscious will, re-centre our lives on God. But being naturally selfish is the same sort of conclusion one comes to from evolutionary theory. Far from discrediting the Adam and Eve story, in this respect at least, evolution serves to throw fresh light on an ancient insight into the intrinsic nature of the human character.

However, this is only part of the story. We find animals sometimes help each other: monkeys grooming each other, for example; hunting in packs rather than trying to go it alone. In these and other situations, there can be survival value in being cooperative rather than aggressive. Biologists call this *reciprocal altruism* – you scratch my back, and I'll scratch yours – literally in the case of those monkeys. So a group of animals might come to arrangements such as: "If you don't steal from me, I won't steal from you"; "I won't try to kill you, if you don't try to kill me"; "I'll leave your mate alone, if you leave mine alone". Arrangements like these are generally to everyone's benefit. It is called "reciprocal altruism", but really it might be more accurately named *"enlightened self-interest"*.

But, of course, don't steal, don't kill, don't commit adultery – which is what such arrangements amount to – are three of the Ten Commandments. So does that not mean that science *is* saying something about where at least certain aspects of morality might come from?

Then there are examples in the animal kingdom of another kind of altruism. It shows itself, for instance, in the way a mother pigeon on seeing a hawk approaching will leave the nest and make a great display, this having the effect of attracting the attention of the predator towards her and away from her helpless young in the nest. This kind of behaviour can be understood in terms of the so-called *selfish gene*. This is the idea that the mother has already passed on her genetic material to her young. In a sense, she has done her job. As far as the genes are concerned, she is now expendable. The genes have a better chance of being passed on further if it is the young that survive rather than the mother. So a gene that in effect says "Whenever it is the case of you or young surviving, always sacrifice yourself" has a better chance of being passed on than one that tells the mother "Always put your own safety first". Such self-sacrificing behaviour is called *altruism on behalf of close kin* – on behalf of those who share the same genetic material.

And again, what holds for animals is thought to throw light on human behaviour. Family ties are strong. There is the well-known mothering instinct whereby mothers especially are inclined to go to great lengths to protect their children and attend to their needs. Such selfless behaviour in humans is regarded as morally good.

Thus, once more, it appears that science, contrary to what we might earlier have thought, does have something to contribute to understanding the way we behave, and why society might encourage certain types of behaviour and not others.

But is that the *whole* story? What about people who give money to the starving overseas – people they are not related to and who cannot pay them back? What about examples of people who pay the supreme sacrifice, surrendering their lives for those who are not close kin? How can we make sense of such acts of self-denial from an evolutionary perspective? Imagine one of our primitive ancestors getting a gene mutation which says "turn the other cheek" or "love your enemies". How long would he or she survive? Is this where religion comes in – with what we might call the *higher* forms of altruism?

Where does the moral sense come from? Is it God-given? Is it man-made?

How far might it be due to evolution through it having survival value?

4 CREATION

- The "six days" creation story helps us understand God's nature, although it doesn't necessarily have to be literally true.

- God's time is different to our own time and therefore the six days described were not physically six days – they're not twenty-four hours each.

- The church's persecution of Galileo for his proposition of a heliocentric universe is just a typical example of organized religion trying to hinder the progression of science.

- Despite the fact that I'm a Catholic myself, I believe that the persecution of Galileo was a shameful episode in the church's history.

- The big bang theory could start everything off and then the six days of creation story quite closely mirrors the process of evolution, the way that goes.

- I believe that the universe began with the big bang, but I do think that does not rule out the existence of God.

- I believe that God created the big bang and evolution was God's way of creating us.

– Why can't we just accept the fact that the
universe is there? Why does there have to be a
creator?

– Scientists have a kind of empirical authority. But
the authority of the Bible is of a higher order.

– I believe that nothing comes from nothing and
that something must have started the big bang
and I think that something is God.

Looking up at the stars on a clear night, we cannot help but
feel a sense of awe and wonder. This is an experience shared
by all peoples since ancient times. But in our modern age it has
been greatly enhanced through the spectacular discoveries of
astronomers and cosmologists. The new horizons so opened up
raise many questions regarding the status of us humans, and
how God is supposed to fit into the whole picture.

Copernicus should probably be credited with having taken the
first step towards a modern understanding of the cosmos. In
1543 he set forth his theory that, contrary to first impressions
seemingly indicating that the Sun is going round the Earth –
the view associated with the Greek philosopher Aristotle – it is
actually the other way round. This suggestion, later backed up
by observations deriving from the newly invented telescope, was
vigorously advocated by Galileo. He presented the arguments
for and against the theory in a book, published in 1632, entitled
Dialogue Concerning the Two Chief World Systems. As the title
indicates, this was written in the form of an imaginary debate.
It involves three participants: Salviati, who speaks for Galileo
in favour of the Copernican heliocentric theory; Simplicio, who
takes the traditional Aristotelian line; and a supposedly impartial
Sagredo. No surprise as to who eventually wins the argument!

As everyone today must surely know, the publication of this
book triggered one of the most shameful episodes in the church's

history. Galileo was put on trial and forced by the church authorities to sign a public recantation:

I Galileo, son of the late Vincenzio Galilei, Florentine, aged seventy years, arraigned personally before this tribunal and kneeling before you, Most Eminent and Lord Cardinals Inquisitors-General against heretical depravity throughout the entire Christian Commonwealth... With sincere heart and apprehended faith I abjure, curse, and detest the aforesaid errors and heresies...

Subsequent accounts of him having been tortured, and indeed having had his eyes put out, were absurd exaggerations. Though he was sentenced to life imprisonment, this was immediately commuted. His punishment was restricted to being put under house arrest and having to recite the seven penitential psalms once a week for three years. Even in this regard, his daughter, who was a Carmelite nun, was allowed to say them on his behalf.

Nevertheless, it remains the case that the whole episode was a disgrace, and it continues to have repercussions, at least in the popular mind, down to the present day. For many, the church's treatment of Galileo is held to be typical of the way religion fights a desperate rearguard action against the progress of science. But is that fair?

The first indication that matters were more complicated than generally realized is the recognition that the book that got Galileo into trouble had in fact passed the church's censors. Next we note that the Pope, Urban VIII, had initially been keen on the project. He was himself most interested in natural philosophy and had written a letter to Galileo congratulating him on the discoveries he had made with his telescope – even writing a poem on the subject. Indeed, the Pope went as far as to insist on having an argument of his own included in the book – something Galileo agreed to do. So what went wrong?

The trouble appears to lie with the way Galileo handled the argument put forward by the Pope. The argument was essentially that God is all-powerful so he could make things *look* as though the Earth was going round the Sun whereas in point of fact it was the Sun going round the Earth. This was supposedly meant as some kind of test of one's faith and reverence for Holy Scripture. It was a fatuous argument, and we can well imagine that Galileo had not been keen on having to include it in what was, after all, a discussion of scientific issues. But the Pope, being the Pope, he had no alternative but to comply. The argument was put into the mouth of Simplicio. Having up to that point in the debate lost on all counts he, as one last desperate throw, puts forward the argument, prefacing it by saying that it is "a most solid doctrine that I once heard from a most eminent and learned person, and before whom one must fall silent...". This could only have meant the Pope himself. Salviati promptly pours withering scorn on the argument, tearing it mercilessly to shreds.

With the benefit of hindsight, and knowing the character of the Pope, this was not a wise thing for Galileo to do! It was this aspect of the book that appears to have been the root cause of the trouble. This became clear some years later when Galileo wrote in a letter:

I hear from Rome that his eminence Cardinal Antonio and the French Ambassador have spoken to his Holiness and attempted to convince him that I never had any intention of committing so sacrilegious an act as to make fun of his Holiness, as my malicious foes have persuaded him and which was the major cause of all my troubles.

"Which was the major cause of all my troubles": there we have it from the mouth of Galileo himself. Contrary to popular opinion, this was not the big science-versus-religion confrontation. Rather it was a petty squabble between an impulsive and overzealous Galileo, and a vain Pope standing on his dignity. If only Galileo had been more tactful, none of the controversy need have happened.

In any case, it is hard to see why a change in cosmological thinking should have been thought so important. After all, the cosmology being defended by the church at the time was not the dominant one to be found in the Bible. That tended to be mainly based on a flat Earth, with heaven above and hell below. The idea of the Earth being a sphere surrounded by spherical shells carrying the Sun, Moon, and stars, with heaven as the furthest shell, was a later idea taken over from Aristotle and his fellow Greek thinkers. The switch from the flat Earth model to the Greek one had been accomplished without any fuss at all. So why should it be such a big deal to have the Earth going round the Sun, rather than the reverse? It might be thought to detract from the supposed importance of humans, but so what? Is not humility regarded as a virtue to be commended?

Leaving the Galileo affair behind, we turn our attention to later developments in astronomy. Just about all of them have served to further downgrade the importance of the Earth in the overall scheme of things. We find that it is but one of eight planets circling the Sun. (It used to be nine before Pluto was relegated for being too small.) The Sun itself is large enough to swallow up a million Earths. And yet it is but a star like all the other stars in the sky – and a medium-sized one at that.

The stars we see, together with many others too faint to be observed with the naked eye, are gathered together into a great swirling whirlpool called the Milky Way galaxy. On a moonless night, away from street lights, we can make out a faint band of light stretching from one horizon to the opposite. In that region of the sky we are looking across to the rest of the galaxy, through the plane of its flattened disc, from our position about two-thirds of the way out from its centre. There are 100 thousand million stars in the Milky Way galaxy.

Our galaxy is not alone. All told there are some 100 thousand million galaxies in the observable universe. That is a lot of stars! Suppose we were to represent each star by a grain of sand. In order to represent all the stars we would need enough sand to build a sandcastle that was five miles long, by five miles wide, by five miles high.

Galaxies are gathered together into clusters, with our own belonging to a cluster of about thirty, known as the Local Group. It is noted that the other clusters are all receding from us. The further away a cluster is, the faster it is retreating into the distance. But why should they be receding from us? Does this mean our own cluster is the centre of the universe? No. The clusters are all receding from each other. So it does not matter to which cluster you belong, all the others seem to be receding from you. Imagine, for example, each cluster is represented by a small coin glued to the surface of a round balloon. As the balloon expands, all the coins move apart. A fly alighting on any one of the coins will see all the others retreating from it.

It is this expansion that provides the first clue as to how the universe came into being. The recessional motion is exactly what would be expected if all the material of the universe had previously been together at a point, and if there had been a great explosion sending the material hurtling outwards. This explosion is called the *big bang*. The motion of the clusters we see today is believed to be the continuing aftermath of that explosion. It was such a catastrophic occurrence, it seems reasonable to conclude that it marked the coming into existence of the universe.

Not that this motion of the clusters can be considered clinching evidence for a big bang. At the time when it was the only indication of an explosive beginning to the universe, not all scientists went along with the notion. There was an alternative theory called the *steady state* theory. This held that if we considered what was happening within a certain volume of space, galaxies would be observed to move out of that region. But, according to this theory, that did not mean the region would become progressively emptier. As the galaxies moved out, their place might be taken by new matter being spontaneously created. This would start out as a thin "soup" of fundamental subatomic particles like neutrons, protons, and electrons. These would collect together to form atoms, the atoms coming together to form stars and planets, which would contribute to forming new galaxies to take the place of those that had retreated from the region. These in their turn would subsequently move out of the region to be replaced by yet more new matter. In other words, the overall picture in that region of space, and in every other region, would, to all intents and purposes, remain looking the same. Hence the name "steady state". Such a universe would have no beginning and no end; it had always existed, and would continue to exist indefinitely. It was an immensely attractive idea. At a stroke, it got rid of the "messy" need for an unexplained one-off explosion occurring at some arbitrary point in time. It was a theory championed in particular by three famous cosmologists: Fred Hoyle, Hermann Bondi, and Tommy Gold.

Now, before you become too enamoured by the charms of this theory, let me hasten to say that it is dead – quite dead! Its demise came about as a result of the acquisition of further observational evidence. Foremost was the detection of *cosmic microwave background radiation*. This is a form of electromagnetic radiation that permeates the whole of space, reaching us from all directions in the sky. It is interpreted as being the cooled-down remnants of the gigantic fireball that accompanied the big bang. It has exactly the frequency spectrum we would expect if it did originate in this way.

Next there is the composition of the interstellar gas. This is largely made up of material thrown out by the big bang and not as yet absorbed into forming stars and planets. On the assumption that there was a big bang, it is possible to calculate what was happening at that time. Subatomic particles – neutrons and protons – were crashing into each other and fusing to form complex atomic nuclei. But then, because of all the violent collisions taking place, most of these would subsequently be broken down again, to be replaced by further fusions. All this would have continued until the expansion had cooled everything down to the point where no more fusions and break-ups could take place – about 100 seconds after the instant of the big bang. This results in what has been called the *freeze-out mix*. Calculations show that the relative abundances of the different elements that make up this mix should consist of about 75 per cent hydrogen by mass, 25 per cent helium, with traces of lithium, and very little else. Sure enough these are the abundances we find in the interstellar gas today.

Finally we mention that, because it takes time for light to reach us from distant objects in the sky, the light we receive from them today was emitted some time in the past. For very distant objects this will be a long time ago. This gives us the opportunity of looking back in time and seeing the universe as it used to be. And what we find is that, contrary to what we expect from the steady state theory, the universe was different in the past to what it is today. For instance, the rate of formation of stars was slower then than it is now. The galaxy clusters were closer together than they are now. In earlier epochs, some galaxies were undergoing violent activities – known observationally as *quasars*. It is believed that the power source of a quasar came from matter being sucked into a supermassive black hole at the centre of a galaxy soon after galaxies first formed. This process has now ceased, there having been no quasars in the last 800 million years.

In this manner, over the years, the case for the big bang has been progressively built up, and we can now say that, among scientific circles, it is almost unanimously accepted. Moreover, we can calculate how long ago the big bang occurred, that is to say, how old the universe is. Knowing the speeds with which the galaxy clusters are moving, and the distances between them and us, we can work out how long it must have taken for them to travel such a distance at that speed. This tells us when they started out; in other words, when the big bang occurred. Our best estimate to date is 13.7 billion years ago. This is nicely consistent with the estimated age of the Earth of 4.5 billion years, as judged from radioactive dating techniques. As we have previously noted, it would of course have taken time for the Earth to form, so we would expect it to have an age less than that of the universe as a whole.

With all this being sewn up so neatly, you might be wondering why I spent any time at all discussing the steady state theory. Part of the reason even today we still sometimes hear questions asked about it. But largely I wanted to draw your attention to the fact that the demise of that theory carries a warning against us being too easily seduced by theories that commend themselves because they are considered aesthetically pleasing. Certainly considerations of simplicity – and indeed beauty – do play a part in guiding scientists to formulate their theories. But at the end of the day, science must always test those theories against hard experimental evidence – a lesson that will play a significant part in our discussion of the relationships between science and religious belief in our final chapter.

So where does all this leave the six-day creation story we find in Genesis? Has the Bible been caught out? As a literal account of how the world came into being, it has always had its problems. The early church leader, Origen (AD 185–254), had this to say:

For who that has understanding will suppose that the first, and second, and third day, and the evening and the morning, existed without a sun, and moon, and stars? and that the first day was, as it were, also without a sky? And who is so foolish as to suppose that God, after the manner of a husbandman, planted a paradise in Eden, towards the east, and placed in it a tree of life...
(Origen, De principiis 4.1.16)

Origen, like St Augustine, was clearly under no illusion that the Genesis creation story should be interpreted in a literal manner – in the way some fundamentalist preachers do today.

Which, as was the case with the Adam and Eve story, is not to say that the Genesis account of the creation of the world has no worth. First of all, it is grounded in the belief that there is but the one God – in itself an important advance on earlier ideas that there was a multiplicity of gods, each with their own characteristics and functions, territorial gods, tribal gods, etc. This single god is in charge of everything. In particular, the world owes its existence to God. Without God there would be nothing. In the memorable phrase coined by the German theologian Paul Tillich, "God is the Ground of all Being".

Though attempts have been made to draw a parallel between the sequence of events described in the six-day story with what happened subsequent to the big bang, these strike many as laboured and unhelpful. It is probably much better to accept the core assertion that, somehow or other, God created the world, the events of the six-day narration being regarded as a form of poetry.

Acceptance of the big bang theory appears to raise an obvious question: What caused it? Here we have to be careful. We observe that everything happening *in* the world has a cause. Boy throws stone – cause; followed by window breaks – effect. But does that necessarily mean that the universe, taken as a whole, has to have a cause? This cautionary warning gains added significance when we consider the *nature* of the expansion of the universe. So far I might have given the impression that the big bang was like any other explosion – bigger, obviously, but essentially the same kind of thing. By that we mean that it took place at a certain point in space, the debris emerging to fill up the surrounding space which had previously been empty. It also took place at some point in time. But physicists do not see things like that. The big bang did not take place at some point in space. There is no call for a blue heritage plaque to be erected at some point in the cosmos declaring "The big bang started here 13.7 billion years BC". Nor did the debris come out and fill up the surrounding space. The galaxy clusters are not receding *through* space; it is space itself that is expanding, and in so doing, carrying the galaxy clusters along with it – much like flotsam floating on the tide. To understand how this comes about, recall once more the coins stuck to the surface of the balloon. As the balloon expands, the coins do not recede from each other by sliding over the rubber surface into areas of rubber where previously there had been no coins. It is the rubber itself that is expanding. And that is how scientists view space – so-called empty space out there; it is a kind of expanding three-dimensional rubber block. Empty space pushing things as heavy as galaxy clusters around. An admittedly counter-intuitive and challenging idea! But that is our best understanding of what is going on.

Next we need to note that space started out as a dot – a point, a region of no volume. In other words, the big bang is believed to mark the coming into existence not only of the contents of the universe, but of space itself. There was no space before the big bang. And when the big bang occurred, there was no space outside the big bang.

That in itself is a remarkable thought. But an even greater surprise is in store for us. According to Einstein's theory of relativity, there is a close connection between space and time – to the extent that the three dimensions of space and the one dimension of time are to be regarded as indissolubly welded together to form a four-dimensional continuum known as *spacetime*. The link is so close that we cannot have space without time, nor time without space. Consequently, it is argued that if the big bang marked the coming into existence of space, it must also have marked the coming into existence of time. There was no time before the big bang.

Now, for those seeking a *cause* of the big bang, this raises a problem. As we have seen, cause is followed by effect. But where the big bang was concerned, there was no before. Thus we cannot have a "cause". Although the question "What caused the big bang?" strikes us as a perfectly reasonable thing to ask, it is not. Our line of argument appears to lead to the conclusion that the question is meaningless.

It was this seeming absence of time before the big bang that prompted the cosmologist Stephen Hawking to pose in his best-seller, *A Brief History of Time*, the rhetorical question: "What place then for a creator?" It certainly gets rid of a god who at some point in time got the idea that he would like to make a world and some creatures he could relate to, and so went ahead, lit the blue touch paper, there was an almighty explosion, and we were on our way. But is that in fact how we should be thinking of God in relation to the creation of the world?

Someone who thought not was St Augustine. Long before modern cosmologists concluded that time might have had a beginning in the big bang, Augustine had already worked out that time was as much a feature of the physical world as any other, and would therefore have had to have been created along with everything else. How did he arrive at that conclusion, given that he, of course, knew nothing about the big bang nor four-dimensional spacetime? He argued as follows: How do we know that there is such a thing as time? It is because things change – the hands of a clock changing their positions in time, for example. But suppose nothing changed, or had ever changed. What would the term "time" refer to? A fortiori, if nothing even existed – changing or not changing – what would the word "time" refer to? Nothing. It would be a meaningless concept. In that simple way, he concluded that time had to be created; it was not something that had some kind of independent existence. That being the case, it was clear to Augustine that God must not be thought of as existing before there was a world – the word "before" signifying a pre-existent time. God is therefore not to be thought of as the "cause" of the world, in the sense that cause comes before effect.

And yet Augustine believed in God the Creator. In order to understand how, we must make a clear distinction between two words which in normal conversation we might use interchangeably, but in theological discourse they must be distinguished. These words are "origins" and "creation". Origins is all about how something gets started – how the world originated. All today's talk about the big bang is to do with origins. As such it has little to do with theology; it is a matter instead for science. Theology, on the other hand, is concerned with creation. It addresses a totally different question, namely "Why is there something rather than nothing?" Why does the world, and ourselves, exist today? Does it take something, or Someone, to keep us in existence? That is why theologians, when addressing questions to do with God as Creator, often couple this with a discussion of God as Sustainer. The creation question is as much concerned with the present moment as with the instant of the big bang.

Strange to say, I find relativity theory helpful in this regard. As already mentioned, physicists like myself regard three-dimensional space and one-dimensional time as indissolubly welded together to form a four-dimensional continuum called spacetime. A crude way of representing spacetime is to extend three fingers and the thumb of one of your hands (keeping the little finger tucked up out of the way). The extended fingers represent the three dimensions of space, and the thumb is the one-dimensional time axis. (This is actually a cheat because all four should be mutually at right angles to each other, which is impossible for us to replicate in our usual three-dimensional space. But if we are not too fussy about angles, this is the best we can do.)

What would we expect to find in spacetime? Clearly it will have to be something characterized by both a position in space and a point in time. We are talking about *events*. One event might consist of you getting tired of reading this book and closing it. It is an event occurring at the position where you are sitting and at some instant in time. As such it will be represented by the point in spacetime having those four coordinates. A second event might take place at a different location, the kitchen, say, at a later instant in time when you plug in the kettle to make a cup of coffee to help keep you awake. That event too will be represented by a point in spacetime. Linking these two points in spacetime will be all the other points representing your progress in going from your seat where you started to where you ended up in the kitchen. This line of points is called your *world line*. (A strange name, I know, but that's what it is called.) In fact your world line stretches right back to the point where and when you were born. Moreover – and this is the difficult part to get our mind round – it extends into the future to the point where and when you die. Your whole life history, from birth to death, is etched into the fabric of spacetime. This, of course, sounds very odd. How can the future exist if it has not yet happened? The trouble with that question is that it assumes that things in spacetime change with time: future events becoming the present before passing into the past. But this is a fallacy. Changes occur in time. But spacetime is not *in* time. On the contrary, time is in *it*. (Recall the thumb of your hand.) Thus nothing changes in spacetime. All of time is there, each instant being on the same footing as every other instant. The fact that spacetime is static is sometimes emphasized by giving the name *the block universe* to all the world lines that make up the complete picture of everything in the universe, past, present, and future.

But if this is the case, you will naturally enough be wondering from where we get the sense of the flow of time – the idea that all that exists is the present, the past has ceased to exist, and the future has yet to exist. The trouble is, no one really knows! It seems somehow to be bound up with consciousness. All we have talked about so far is how the physicist describes the physical world. But we have not said anything about how we, as conscious *mental* beings, perceive that physical world. Conscious awareness of the world is sometimes described as being like a searchlight beam that picks out a particular point in physical time and labels it "the present". Having done so, it immediately moves on to the next point, progressively scanning along the time axis.

You will now, of course, object: How can it "move on"? Does not that change of position of the searchlight beam indicate that, contrary to what I have just said, something *is* changing in the block universe – changing in time? Here we have to acknowledge that according to some philosophers we are dealing with not one, but two distinct types of time. The need for a second type of time becomes apparent when we consider the meaning of the phrase "the flow of time". This flow is something familiar to us all. We experience time marching on in a dynamic fashion. Moreover it appears to progress at different paces. When bored we speak of time as "dragging". As we get older time seems to fly. But what do we mean by "a flow"? A flow is a change of something in a given time. The flow of a river is a measure of how much water passes a particular position in a given time. But what is a flow of time? The amount of time that has passed in a given time? What can that possibly mean? Nothing – not unless we are talking of *two* types of time. How much of Time 1 has passed in a given amount of Time 2.

To see how this might make sense, note the time on a clock or watch. Then close your eyes. After a while try to estimate how much time has passed. Open your eyes and compare this mental estimate with the new reading on the clock. Sometimes you will overestimate, and sometimes underestimate. If you overestimated, then it appears that time is dragging – the hands of the clock appear to have been going slow. And vice versa.

This comes about because you are comparing a physical time interval – as recorded on the clock and etched into the fabric of the block universe – with an interval of consciously perceived mental time. According to this way of viewing matters, if there were no conscious beings having mental experiences, the flow of time would be a meaningless concept. All we would be left with is the static block universe.

In all fairness, I should perhaps point out that although I personally go along with this viewpoint, there are scientists – highly respected physicists – who do not. They accept that the concept of spacetime is a useful, and indeed perhaps an indispensable, aid towards accounting for various features of the world – those features addressed by relativity theory – it might, nevertheless, be no more than a mathematical device for making calculations, rather than being a reflection of how the physical world actually is.

But let us suppose, for the sake of argument, that the block universe is real. To understand why I have been at such pains to describe it to you, look once more at the extended fingers and thumb representing the block universe. Imagine it containing all the world lines constituting the whole story of the universe. From your privileged position outside the hand you can, at a glance, take in the whole picture: past, present, and future. This is the best representation I can give you of how a theologian might understand God in relation to the world. We sometimes talk of God in this regard as being *transcendent*. This means he is beyond space and time. He takes it all in. The past and the future are as vivid and real to God as the present. This is why it is commonly held that God has foreknowledge. He knows the future before we mental beings consciously experience it. Which is not to say that God lies exclusively outside of spacetime. Though he has this "extra dimensional" viewpoint, God is also to be found *in* the world. We speak of God as being *immanent* as well as being transcendent. When we pray to God, for instance, we are interacting with God in this immanent sense.

I have said how all the events that make up the story of the world are etched into the fabric of spacetime. One way of looking at it is to say that it constitutes God's "home movie". With a home movie we are viewing a record of ourselves engaged in some activity – a holiday, for example. In the same way God, in his transcendent capacity, can view himself in action within the world.

With all this in mind, let us return to the question of God the Creator, and the distinction we have tried to make between the two words "origins" and "creation". We ask: "If God is to create a physical world – a block universe in which all instants of time are on an equal footing – why would he take a particular interest in the instant marking one end of the world lines – namely that representing the big bang?" It could be argued that that instant is no more significant than any other. It has to be the whole ensemble, or nothing. It is in this sense we say that God is the answer to the question of why there is something rather than nothing, and how the world is sustained in existence.

Not that Stephen Hawking would agree. We saw earlier how in his book *A Brief History of Time* he confused the question of origins with that of creation. For this he was taken to task by various critics. In his later book, *The Grand Design*, he claims to have taken these objections on board and has indeed now successfully answered the question of why there is something rather than nothing. His answer? *M-theory*. This is the suggestion that there might be a law of nature, the function of which is to spontaneously produce universes – producing them out of nothing. The workings of this law of nature gave rise to this universe, and to many others. The whole ensemble of universes is given the name *multiverse*.

But, you might ask, how can we get something out of nothing – whether we are thinking of M-theory or God? Actually it is not as difficult as you might think! Take, for instance, electric charge. In my own research work we create electric charge out of nothing all the time. We smash tiny subatomic particles (protons or electrons) together in high energy collisions and we create new subatomic particles. Some of these new particles carry electric charge that was not there before the collision. How do we do it? The trick is to recognize that, as everyone knows, there are two types of charge: positive and negative. So whenever we create a positively charged particle, we at the same time create another particle carrying an equal amount of negative charge. That way, the *net* amount of charge is not altered and the law of conservation of electric charge is upheld.

But now you might ask where the new particles themselves come from – the particles carrying the new amounts of charge. They were created out of the energy of motion (kinetic energy) of the original colliding particles. This is a consequence of Einstein's famous equation $E = mc^2$, where E stands for energy and m for mass (c is the speed of light and has to be included in the equation so as to get the units right). This holds that energy and mass are equivalent. As you are doubtless aware, energy comes in different forms: heat energy, gravitational energy, electrical energy, kinetic energy, potential energy, and so on. Matter is yet another form of energy – a kind of locked-up form of energy. Contrary to the maxim "matter can be neither created nor destroyed", it can indeed be created, provided you are prepared to lose some other form of energy in the process. Following upon one of these high energy collisions, we find the creation of these new particles is accompanied by a corresponding loss of the kinetic energy of the original bombarding particles. And the process can occur in reverse. The heat and light energy given out by the Sun results from nuclear reactions that entail a reduction in the amount of matter.

If all the matter we see around us is a form of energy, that in turn raises the question as to where all this energy came from.

Here we need to recognize that, like electric charge, energy can be both positive and negative. Take, for example, a proton and an electron isolated from each other. As we have seen, they have energy by virtue of their masses. Put the two together to form an atom of hydrogen, and we find that it takes energy to pull them apart again. Therefore the bound system has less energy than the two isolated particles. The atom has the energy characteristic of the masses of the two particles, minus the binding energy (i.e. the energy that would have to be supplied in order to pull them apart). This introduces an ambiguity as to what we should take as the zero level of energy. There is clearly a great deal of positive energy contained in all the matter of the universe and in its energy of motion. But everything is exerting a gravitational attraction on everything else, thus giving rise to negative binding energy. If, as a thought experiment, we were somehow to remove an object away from the entire universe (which, of course, we could not!) it could be argued that it might require all of its locked-up internal energy to overcome its binding energy to the universe. In other words, its net energy (locked-up energy minus binding energy) might be exactly zero. And the same goes for everything else. The net energy of the universe might well be zero.

The same goes for other properties such as momentum. Momentum is a property of moving objects. It is a directional quantity. But because there are as many objects (galaxies, say) moving in one direction as another, the net momentum of the universe as a whole is zero. Spinning objects like the Sun and the Earth possess a property called angular momentum. But there are as many objects in the universe spinning clockwise as there are spinning anticlockwise, so the net result is again nothing.

Thus it is conjectured that the entire universe might add up to precisely nothing – albeit an ingenious rearrangement of the original nothing! Which brings us to the question of how to bring about this rearrangement. According to Hawking, the answer is M-theory rather than God. The launch of his book setting out this claim caused quite a stir at the time. We noted in the Introduction that the news prompted a banner headline in *The Times* newspaper, no less. The book proclaimed that philosophy was dead (though it was pointed out by at least one reviewer that his text was permeated throughout with philosophical statements). Theology was also to be discounted. He went on to claim that "scientists have become the bearers of the torch of discovery in our quest for knowledge". M-theory was hailed as "a candidate for the ultimate theory of everything... the only candidate". The book ends with the statement "... we will have found the grand design." Which might strike us as odd. According to my dictionary, a design is something that is planned and has a purpose; it requires a designer. This appears to hold open the back door for God to come in – which I am sure was not the author's intention.

So from all this, did Hawking succeed in answering the creation question in a manner that excludes God? The simple answer is no. Though M-theory might indeed account for the mechanism by which our universe (and possibly others) originated, it in turn raises the question of where M-theory is supposed to have come from – meaning M-theory itself.

Indeed, this is part of a wider question concerning the laws of nature in general. The laws are intelligible. We have to use our intelligence to recognize them and formulate them. That being so, might it be argued that it could have taken an Intelligence to have set them up in the first place?

What does M-theory look like? Is it neat and tidy like $E = mc^2$, or is it complicated, filling the whole of a blackboard – as so often depicted in Hollywood films showing scientists supposedly at work? No one knows. It has yet to be formulated. At the present stage it is but a gleam in the eye. There is not even a consensus as to what the "M" might stand for. It could be "membrane", "matrix", or "mother" (as in "the mother of all theories"). More tongue-in-cheek suggestions have been "monster", "mystery", and "magic".

One of the attractions of M-theory, should there be such a theory, is that it is in a sense a steady state type of theory. The idea is that you have a universe. A region within that universe undergoes a big bang and produces a daughter universe. This offspring could have completely different characteristics to its parent universe. The masses of the fundamental particles could be different, the strengths of the various forces, the violence of its big bang origin, etc. It might even have its own time and space. The daughter universe in her turn can spawn granddaughter universes, and so on. Where did the original universe come from? That is held to have arisen from a yet earlier universe, and so on indefinitely in that direction of time too. In other words, this succession of universes has no beginning and no end – like the original steady state theory we discussed earlier.

On the assumption that M-theory is true, it is difficult, if not impossible, to see how it is to be verified. How are we supposed to demonstrate that universes other than our own exist? We might think that we have only to travel far enough out into space to come across the boundary between our universe and the next one. Unfortunately, even our nearest neighbour universe would be much, much too far away. Moreover it would be receding from us at a speed faster than light, so we would never have a chance of catching up with it. Thus it appears impossible directly to prove that such a universe is out there, let alone examine it to see if its laws of nature are different from ours.

The hope has to be that there might be some features of this universe that are indicative that there might be the others. But doesn't that mean the scientist is liable to find him or herself in the position of religious believers today trying to decide whether there is a heavenly realm or not? Denied access to such a realm (for the time being at least), they have to rely on indirect clues in this material world that might point to the conclusion that there could be more beyond – evidence such as the reported resurrection of Jesus, answers to prayer, religious experiences, etc.

On the assumption that the theory is correct, and that our universe is part of a multiverse, how would that impact on religious belief? As you might expect from what has gone before, the lack of a beginning, or origin, to the multiverse would not impinge at all on the creation question. Nevertheless, are we to regard M-theory as an implacable rival to the God hypothesis? Not necessarily. M-theory could be regarded as God's way of producing this universe, as well as others. God sets up the law; the law is then responsible for bringing the multiverse into being on his behalf.

Having dealt at some length with how we think the universe might have originated, let us end with just a word about how we expect it all to end. It is anticipated that the expansion of the universe will go on for ever. The stars will eventually exhaust all their fuel. Some will swell up to become *red giants*. In the case of our Sun, this is expected to occur some 5 billion years from now. Mercury and Venus will be swallowed up. The fiery surface is, however, unlikely to reach as far as Earth. But no matter. The temperature here will be so hot as to end all life. Thereafter, the remains of the Sun will sink down to become a *white dwarf*, before fizzling out. The same fate awaits all similar sized stars. Heavier ones will end their lives spectacularly with a *supernova explosion*. Briefly, this one star will outshine all the others in its galaxy, before leaving behind a black hole. It is then expected that the remnants of all the stars making up a galaxy will eventually be drawn together to form a supermassive black hole. This in turn will gradually evaporate, leaving a very dilute gas expanding for ever. The universe will become dark and cold. This is called the *heat death of the universe*. And, of course, that will be the end of life everywhere. A rather gloomy prediction – one that some people interpret as a challenge to religious belief.

Does it not indicate that the universe is meaningless; it has no ultimate purpose?

If this mortal life is all that there is, then this indeed is a powerful argument. Life would be devoid of any overall purpose, other than what we ourselves might endue it with. However, most of the major religions emphatically do not regard this mortal life as being what really matters. In the context of eternal life, this life is but "a vale of soul-making", as the poet John Keats put it in a letter he once wrote. The universe is the mould in which our spiritual selves develop. And it is these spiritual selves that count. Once these are formed, the universe is, in a sense, expendable; it has done its job. Indeed, by analogy with the production of bronze sculptures, once the required number have been created, the original mould can be broken. In fact, it is often deliberately broken to underline the fact that this particular sculpture comes in a limited edition. The individual examples are more valued the smaller the edition.

This end to all life assumes that there is but the one universe. In the case of a multiverse, there is presumably a continual production of new life. As fast as one universe suffers a heat death, others come into existence through the continuing operation of M-theory and new life is created – at least in those universes that satisfy all the conditions necessary for a universe to be able to support life – the subject of our next chapter.

In the light of our modern understanding of cosmology, is it still possible to think of a Creator God?

If not, what else could be the answer to the question: "Why is there something rather than nothing?"

5 THE ANTHROPIC PRINCIPLE

- The universe is hostile to life – the depths
  of space are freezing cold, planets are
  inhospitable, and the sun's just a blazing fire.
  So if God was intending to create a home for
  life why would he create it in such a hostile
  environment?

- The vastness of the universe fascinates me,
  but I'm not overwhelmed by it. I think it's just an
  indication of how powerful God really is.

- The vastness of the universe doesn't detract
  from the importance of humans. If anything it
  makes us more important, because out of all of
  the space we've got life and I think that that's a
  miracle.

- I think that God created the universe to be a
  home for humans, for animals, for everything
  else he created.

- Life is an accidental by-product of chance – it
  has no intrinsic purpose and therefore it's down
  to us alone to give it purpose.

- I think there's a multiverse – an infinite number
  of universes, some with life and some not. The
  fact that we are here is not all that amazing.

– With the belief in a multiverse one can draw a
  parallel with a belief in heaven and hell which
  also cannot be seen. Scientists have to have
  faith too.

From time immemorial, religious people have held that we
humans have a special relationship with God. The world was
made by God as a home for us. But that view has been challenged
by, among others, Steven Weinberg, the Nobel Prize-winning
physicist. In his best-selling book *The First Three Minutes*, he
declares: "The more the universe is comprehensible, the more
it also seems pointless." He goes on to dismiss human life as "a
more or less farcical outcome of a chain of accidents".

It is not difficult to see how he arrives at such a pessimistic
conclusion. For a start, consider the immensity of the universe.
We have seen how it contains a vast number of stars: 100 billion
in our Milky Way galaxy; 100 billion galaxies. And that simply
accounts for the galaxies within our observable universe – within
the limits of what we can see as set by the time it takes light to
reach us from them since the big bang. Beyond the observable
universe there presumably lies the rest of the universe. Each
star, as we have seen, is a sun much like our own Sun. A large
proportion of them are known to have planetary systems similar
to our own Solar System.

All of this takes up a great deal of space. Our galaxy is fairly
typical of the larger galaxies. It is so big that it takes 100,000
years for light to cross from one side of it to the other – this
despite the fact that light travels at a speed of 300,000 kilometres
(or 186,000 miles) per second. We say that the diameter of our
galaxy is 100,000 light years. As for the observable universe
taken as a whole, it has taken 13.7 billion years for light to reach
us from its furthest extremities. And beyond that, the rest of the
universe might extend indefinitely. A home for us humans? The
sceptic might well feel this was a case of over-design!

How about the contents of the universe? The most prominent objects are the stars. These are great balls of fire – nuclear bombs going off slowly. Clearly not a home for life. For there to be life, it must evolve on a planet going round a star. It needs the energy poured out by the star in order to sustain the process. But get too close to the star – like Mercury or Venus – and conditions are too hot. Further out, conditions are too cold. The vast reaches of outer space are freezing. So, like the porridge in the story of Goldilocks and the three bears, the temperature of the planet has to be just right. And it is not only a question of getting the temperature right. The outer planets, Jupiter, Saturn, Neptune, and Uranus, are largely made up of hydrogen and helium gas. They might have a small, hot rocky core. Nevertheless, they clearly are not the kind of places where we expect to find life. And as with our Solar System, it is expected that the majority of planets orbiting other stars will not be hospitable for life.

With all this in mind, it is easy to conclude, along with Weinberg, that the universe is basically hostile to life, and we humans are but a freak of nature. And yet first impressions can be misleading. Since the early 1970s there has been the growing realization that there is something very strange about the universe. The deeper we enquire into it, the more life-friendly it seems to be – to the extent that we even hear it said that it appears to have been fine-tuned to produce life.

Take, for example, the size of the universe. Yes, it is big. But in order to accommodate us, it *had* to be big. It took 9 billion years for the Solar System to form, and then a further 4.5 billion years for evolution to produce us. During all that time the universe was expanding – and at the speed of light. Keep that up for that length of time and the universe ends up big. We could not look out on a universe that was any smaller.

But, you might ask, why should the universe expand at such a seemingly excessive speed? At this point we need briefly to consider not just the degree of violence of the big bang, but the whole chain of events that led to us putting in our appearance on the scene. Having done that, we shall look back on that history and see in how many different ways it could all have gone wrong as far as the eventual development of life was concerned.

We begin with the big bang. Out from it came subatomic particles: protons, neutrons, helium nuclei, electrons, and packets of electromagnetic or light energy called *photons*. After 380,000 years everything had cooled down to 3,000 K (about 2,700 °C), a temperature low enough for the electrons to attach themselves to the nuclei to form the first atoms. This went to make up clouds of gas. Those regions of gas that happened to be denser than average exerted a gravitational attraction on the surrounding gas, drawing it in to form even denser regions. In doing so, these pockets of gas heated up, in much the same way that air being squashed into a bicycle pump heats up. If enough gas is collected and compressed, the temperature can reach several million degrees, at which point nuclear fusion can take place, and a star is born. Protons carry positive electric charge and the repulsive electric force so produced can make it difficult for them to approach each other. But at these high temperatures, where the protons collide violently with each other, they can get in close enough for the short-ranged, attractive nuclear force to take over and bind them together to form larger nuclei. It is a process that releases vast amounts of energy: the energy of *nuclear fusion*. These nuclei are those that will eventually make up the wide variety of different types of atom needed later to form rocky planets such as the Earth, and also the material of our bodies. It is quite a thought that everything that makes up our bodies was once in the depths of a star at a temperature of millions of degrees! We are made of stardust (or, depending on our point of view, nuclear waste).

But, having made all this material in that hostile environment, how was it to be got out into space? That is where the supernovae come in – those great explosions that mark the death of particularly massive stars. A proportion of its material is blasted out into space. Here it joins up with the rest of the interstellar gas – the hydrogen and helium that came out of the big bang and as yet has not been incorporated into a star. This "contaminated" gas now condenses down to form later generations of stars. But because of the "contamination" there is an important difference. Though some of the planets around the new star will be gaseous (like Jupiter, Saturn, etc.) some will now be rocky – like the Earth or Mars. The fact that our Solar System has such rocky planets goes to show that our Sun is a later generation star. With the formation of the Earth occurring at a distance from the Sun that gives it a temperate climate, the stage is now set for the process of evolution by natural selection to commence.

Such is the quick run-down of our history. Now let us retrace our steps and, as I said earlier, take account of where it could have all gone wrong as far as living creatures being able eventually to put in an appearance is concerned.

In the first place, we have to consider the violence of the original big bang. We need to take into account that everything emerging from it will be attracting everything else with the force of gravity. As the distances grow, so this force will diminish (remember the inverse square law of attraction), but it will still persist to even the largest distances. There will therefore be a tendency for everything to slow down, although that tendency will diminish with time. The question then arises as to whether this slowing down will be sufficient to bring everything to a halt at some future time. If so, with the gravitational attraction still being felt, the tendency afterwards would be for everything to be drawn back together again in what has been colourfully named the *big crunch*. If, on the other hand, the gravitational attraction is not sufficient to bring everything to a halt, then the expansion will continue for ever.

So which scenario will it be? It all depends upon the average density of matter and energy in the universe. The higher the density, the stronger will be the mutual gravitational attraction. There will be a special value of the density, called the *critical density*, which marks the boundary between the two cases. It turns out that the density of the universe is measured to be very close to the critical value. A coincidence? Not really. In order for the density today to be so close to that value, it means that at the instant of the big bang it would have had to have been extremely close to the critical value. If it had been the slightest bit less, then the difference would have been greatly magnified by now – and similarly if it had been marginally more than critical, by today it would have been much greater than critical. It must have started out as exactly critical. In fact, this is believed to be the case. It is now accepted that a tiny fraction of a second after the instant of the big bang, there was a brief period of exceedingly rapid expansion called *inflation*. It is not appropriate for me in a book like this to go into the details as to why we should think this. But inflation theory is now generally accepted among cosmologists. One of its important characteristics is that it leads to a universe where the density after the inflationary period is exactly critical.

This being so, we are led to think how fortunate this is for us humans and all other forms of life. Inflation theory ensured that the universe was not one of high density leading to a big crunch – an end to the universe before we were able to come onto the scene. But then we have to consider the opposite effect: namely, the universe expanding too fast for the gases emerging from the big bang to be able to collect together to form stars before they had separated too far. Here we come across a recent discovery. Searches were carried out involving very distant galaxy clusters to try to ascertain to what degree the clusters were slowing down under the influence of their mutual gravity. To everyone's surprise, it was found that whereas the clusters had indeed slowed down initially, they were now speeding up! The very distant clusters were actually accelerating away from us. This is because of something called *dark energy*. It is a property of space itself. It permeates all of space. As the universe expands and more and more space is created, so there is more and more dark energy to go along with that extra space. The interesting thing about this dark energy is that it exerts a force. It is a force of repulsion, and as such behaves like a form of anti-gravity. So what we find is that there is now so much space – and hence dark energy – in the universe that we have gone over from the initial gravity-induced slowing down to the dark-energy-induced speeding up.

This dark energy is believed to arise out of all the kinds of processes physicists believe could be going on in so-called empty space (processes that arise out of quantum physics – which again we need not go into). Having recognized that these processes would produce a repulsive force of their own, the surprise for physicists is not that the force is there, but that it is so feeble. Their expectation is that it should be 120 orders of magnitude greater (that is a factor of 1 followed by 120 noughts). It is all rather embarrassing! But what a good thing it is that this repulsive force is as weak as it is. If it had been much stronger, it would have blown away all the gas from the big bang before it had a chance to collect together to form stars – and without stars, there could have been no life.

Having successfully negotiated two potential pitfalls – the big crunch and the alternative too-rapid dispersal of material due to the force exerted by dark energy – do we now have our stars? Not really. I said how in order for stars to form there had to be regions in the gas from the big bang that were denser than other regions. These were to act as the seeds for the growth of the stars. If the gas had been completely uniform there would have been no reason why the gas should condense at one place rather than any other. It would have remained essentially diffuse before spreading out indefinitely, becoming ever more dilute. Thus, the gaseous medium had to have a certain "graininess" to it. This, in fact, can be investigated by examining the cosmic microwave background radiation. As we have previously noted, this is the radiation left over from the big bang. Studying it gives us a glimpse of the universe at a very early stage. At first sight, the radiation is uniform across the sky. It is uniform to one part in 100,000. But more detailed study reveals slight variations. Certain regions are hotter than others. These come about because the matter emitting the radiation was not absolutely uniform in density. Thus, the radiation gives us clues as to the early inhomogeneities present in the medium – those that were later to act as the centres upon which the stars and galaxies formed. But, of course, it is easy to imagine a situation where these inhomogeneities were insufficient to lead to such condensations. In which case, we would again have had no stars. If the inhomogeneities were more pronounced, we would have encountered a different kind of problem. We would have had our stars, but now they would have found themselves in more densely packed galaxies. Close encounters with near neighbouring stars would have led to the disruption of planetary systems. There would not have been the settled, long-term conditions necessary for the slow processes of evolution to reach the stage where intelligent life developed.. Getting the right degree of graininess was a third hurdle we successfully negotiated.

So now we have our stars, and the fusion of nuclei needed later for the heavier types of atom can begin. Fusion occurs because there is this very strong force of attraction between protons and neutrons. This so-called *strong nuclear force* is, as we have said, short-ranged, so the particles have to get in close to each other before they feel its effects. First of all hydrogen, consisting of a single proton, has to be converted into helium, characterized by having two protons in its nucleus. But two protons on their own cannot combine because of the electrostatic repulsion exerted by their positive electric charges. But this is not a problem for a proton and a neutron – the neutron carrying no electric charge, and therefore being able to get in close. The proton and neutron can combine to form deuterium – a heavier form of hydrogen. The deuterium provides a stepping stone for the formation of helium, which is made up of two protons and two neutrons. It is the extra attractive strong nuclear force exerted by the neutrons that provides the extra "glue" to hold the two protons together despite the continuing tendency of their electric charges to push them apart. And the same is true of the heavier nuclei that will later be formed: we need the additional attractive forces exerted by neutrons to hold the nucleus together.

However, there are no free neutrons knocking around in the interstellar gas out of which the stars form. Yes, neutrons were emitted from the big bang, but neutrons on their own are unstable; in about twenty minutes they decay to a proton, electron, and a neutrino. So neutrons have somehow to be created within the star. Fortunately there is a type of interaction whereby a proton, in the course of colliding with another proton, effectively changes back into a neutron. This is a comparatively slow process, which is a good thing from our point of view because it prolongs the overall active life of the star, to the extent that it gives enough breathing space for evolution to take place on a nearby planet – another condition that needed to be satisfied.

The helium nucleus weighs 99.3 per cent of the mass of its four constituent particles. The remaining 0.7 per cent appears as the energy release of the nuclear fusion – the energy radiated by the star. As you might expect, this percentage is governed by the strength of the nuclear force binding the protons and neutrons. But what if the strength of the nuclear force had been different? Suppose it had been less, giving rise to, let us say, a 0.6 per cent reduction. The reduced nuclear force would have meant that the proton and neutron would not have formed a stable bound system. Without deuterium as an intermediate stage, the pathway to helium would be blocked. The world today would simply consist of the original hydrogen coming out of the big bang. There would be no heavier elements, no rocky planets, and no us.

What if the nuclear force had been stronger, giving rise, say, to a mass reduction of 0.8 per cent instead of the 0.7 per cent? Now we would find that two protons would have been able to bind together without the need for additional neutrons. And this combination of protons would have happened during the big bang itself, to the extent that no hydrogen would have been emitted. There would have been no nuclear fuel left over for the generation of heat in stars, and without a sun, there could be no life on neighbouring planets. In other words, for there to be life in the universe, the strength of the nuclear force has to be what it is – neither more nor less. Was this simply a coincidence?

But even with the strength of the nuclear force being what we needed it to be, we come across an additional problem. An especially important kind of atom is carbon. We might regard it as a very "sticky" kind of atom. It is the basic building block for assembling the large complicated molecules characteristic of organic life – the DNA molecule, for example. The nucleus of a carbon atom essentially consists of a bound system of three helium nuclei. First we have two helium nuclei coming together and producing a nucleus of beryllium. Then along comes the third helium nucleus to attach itself to the other two. So what is the problem? The trouble is that the beryllium nucleus thus formed is unstable. It rapidly breaks up again, in about 10^{-17} second (i.e. a fraction of a second equal to 1 divided by one 100,000 million million). Before the third helium nucleus can get there, its target nucleus is no more. Thus, it is impossible to produce carbon – and we humans should not be here! Except, of course, we are here. But how?

It was the cosmologist Fred Hoyle who came up with the solution. He claimed that the answer must be a *nuclear resonance*. Let me explain: A peculiar property of subatomic particles is that when they approach each other, how likely they are to hit each other can depend on their approach speed. At certain speeds, they have a much better chance than usual of interacting with each other. It is as though they look bigger to each other. This phenomenon is called a "nuclear resonance". Hoyle argued that, at the typical speeds we find in a star, the beryllium nucleus and approaching helium nucleus must have struck one of these nuclear resonances. The beryllium nucleus looks enormous to the helium nucleus, and this greatly increases the chances of the two colliding and sticking together to form the precious carbon before the unstable particle is due to disintegrate. He suggested that experiments in the laboratory should be carried out to test this conjecture. His suggestion was at first greeted with scepticism. After all, nobody before had ever had the temerity to try to *predict* where we would find such a resonance. But in due course the experiment was carried out and the resonance was found. The mystery of the formation of carbon was solved. But what a close run thing. Without that resonance being there, we would not be here. Hoyle was in later life to declare:

A common sense interpretation of the facts suggests that a super intellect has monkeyed with physics, as well as with chemistry and biology, and that there are no blind forces worth speaking about in nature. The numbers one calculates from the facts seem to me so overwhelming as to put this conclusion almost beyond question.
("The Universe: Past and Present Reflections", 1981)

I once heard Hoyle speak along these lines. After his lecture I spoke to him. I was puzzled. Hoyle had the reputation for being a confirmed atheist, this having been made clear during a controversial series of BBC radio broadcasts he had given in 1950 entitled *The Nature of the Universe*. These had been devoted to setting out the case for the steady state theory as opposed to that of the big bang. The idea that the universe had always existed in this steady state he claimed ruled out a Creator God. I reminded him of those broadcasts and asked whether, in the light of what he was now saying, he had changed his mind. He was quick to deny that he had anything to do with *organized* religion. "Fair enough," I replied, "but have you changed your mind about God?" Rather grudgingly he admitted, "Yes."

Having got our carbon, is the stage now set to produce life? Hardly. We have the raw materials, but where are they? They are in a furnace at a temperature of millions of degrees. Somehow we have to get them out. But how? They are, in fact, ejected by supernova explosions. As we saw earlier, these occur when giant stars reach the end of their active life and begin to run out of nuclear fuel. As energy continues to be lost through the star's surface, but not so much is now being produced, the temperature starts to dip. The motion of the star's constituents is no longer so violent. It was this agitation that had been responsible for the star being able to hold itself up under the crushing force of its own gravity. But with this resistance weakening, gravity gets a stronger grip, to the point where the star undergoes catastrophic collapse. The electrons and protons are compacted together so close they fuse to form neutrons. This becomes the core of what is left: a *neutron star.* This is the fate of certain massive stars; they are reduced to a small rapidly spinning ball of neutrons. But for the really big stars that is not the end of the story. For them, gravity becomes so strong that even this neutron core cannot withstand its own gravitational force, and it collapses down to a point. Thus is formed a black hole.

All this was well understood. What puzzled astrophysicists for years was not so much why stars collapse, but how this process gave rise to an explosion. How could an *im*plosion give rise to an *ex*plosion? The answer was later found to be the strangest possible. The outer layer of material of the star was being blasted out by neutrinos. These were being produced when the electrons and protons merged to form the neutrons of the neutron core.

Neutrinos are famous for hardly interacting with anything. Our Sun is continually pouring out neutrinos, to the extent that 100,000 billion of them pass through your body every second. Yet you do not feel a thing. This is because they are so slippery, only one or two are likely to scatter off you in your lifetime. However, the extraordinary thing is that it was neutrinos that ejected from a star the material that makes up your body. A supernova explosion produces 1,000 times as many neutrinos as our Sun will produce in its 10 billion year lifetime. And it is this extremely dense flux of neutrinos that made all the difference. But does this not give us further pause for reflection? What if neutrinos had been even more slippery than they are? And, for that matter, what if they had been more strongly reacting? In this latter case, they would have interacted with the lower lying layers of the star and would not have had enough energy on reaching the surface to eject the outer layer. Again we appear to have struck it lucky.

So, now we have the material safely out in space away from the furnace in which it was forged. It collects together to form our later generation Sun, together with its planets, including the Earth which is to be our home. Evolution is now able to take over. This, of course, is to be a long drawn-out process. The Earth needs to keep orbiting the Sun for this length of time. Obviously. But even this is not as straightforward as we might suppose. The Earth must maintain a stable orbit. It remains in orbit because the tendency it has to fly off into space in a straight line – the centrifugal effect – is exactly balanced by its gravitational attraction to the Sun. The strength of this attraction falls off with distance according to the inverse square law. Objects at twice the distance experience a quarter of the force; ten times the distance, one hundredth of the force. This inverse square law arises because the surface area of a sphere increases as the radius, r, squared ($A = 4\pi r^2$ to be precise). That in turn means that twice the distance away from the centre, the gravitational force is spread out over four times the area. We can think of it as being "diluted" by that factor. What is true of the gravitational force is also the case for the electrostatic force produced by an electric charge. It too obeys an inverse square law, and for the same reason.

Such a dependence of the gravitational force is extremely fortunate for us. It means that if the Earth were to get slightly shifted out of its orbit (by a meteorite impact, for instance), it would gently adopt a slightly different orbit. If it were to find itself slightly closer to the Sun, it would experience a certain increase in the centrifugal force. But this would be exactly balanced by the stronger gravitational force at this reduced distance. Thus it could carry on as though nothing special had occurred. Not so were the restraining force to obey some other law – an inverse cube law, for example, where a doubling of the distance would mean that the gravitational force would reduce by a factor of 8, rather than 4. Were that to be the case, a slight slowing down of the Earth would mean it would move into a region where the force was considerably stronger, and it would spiral down into the Sun. On the other hand, if the meteorite impact caused it to speed up a little, it would move out to a region where the force was significantly less, and the Sun would lose its grip on us, and the Earth would drift off into outer space. We say that, under these conditions, the Earth's orbit would be unstable.

But, you might be thinking, dreaming up an imaginary inverse cube law is being a bit fanciful. Why should there be such a dependence? The answer is all to do with the number of spatial dimensions. In this world there are, of course, three spatial dimensions (plus one-dimensional time). But had there been four spatial dimensions, the area of a "sphere" would depend on the radius cubed, and we would indeed have gravitational and electrostatic forces with an inverse cube dependence.

The same applies to all higher spatial dimensions; orbits would be unstable. There would be no long-lived planets where life had a chance to evolve. So, for there to be life, there must not be more than three spatial dimensions. As for the case of a two-dimensional world, the problems of having life as we know it in such an environment was explored way back in 1884 by Edwin Abbott in his amusing book *Flatland*. Thus we conclude that yet a further condition for the development of life is that there should have been three spatial dimensions – no more and no fewer.

So we have a stable planet on which evolution can take place. This is a process that takes energy, and that energy source is, of course, the Sun. It is needed to give warmth; it is needed for the growth of vegetation to provide food, etc. It has to be a steady source of energy, functioning for a very long time, namely 4.5 billion years.

It is at this point we need to recognize just what a remarkable phenomenon the Sun is. After all, it is a nuclear bomb going off slowly! Ever since humans on planet Earth invented hydrogen bombs, strenuous efforts have been made to harness all that energy for peaceful purposes. The current generation of nuclear power stations is based on the break-up, or fission, of heavy nuclei. This entails problems of getting adequate supplies of fuel, uranium, and leaves us with a legacy of radioactive waste that has somehow to be disposed of. Power stations based on the fusion of light nuclei, as in the Sun, would offer an altogether more attractive prospect. The energy release of fusion is much greater than that of fission (compare the destructive power of the fission bombs used in World War II with that of the hydrogen fusion bombs developed later). There would be a limitless supply of fuel – the deuterium to be found in sea water. And radioactive waste would not be a problem. Yet despite all these efforts, dating back to the 1950s, none of the electricity you use in the home comes from this source. The technical difficulties are immense. The problem is largely that of holding the exceedingly hot interacting matter (called a *plasma*) in a confined space under conditions where, because of the extreme temperature, it cannot be allowed to touch any walls, which would instantly melt. The confinement is carried out by magnetic fields. Great strides have been made in overcoming the difficulties, but there is still a long way to go.

On the other hand, we have the Sun up there in the heavens doing it effortlessly for nothing! A steady source of energy for the past 5 billion years, with another 5 billion to go. How does it do it? We have already noted that the conversion of protons into neutrons in the core of the Sun is a slow process. But that is just one feature contributing to the Sun's longevity. In order for the Sun to burn steadily over such a long period of time, there has to be a delicate balance between the rate at which heat is generated by the fusion processes taking place in the Sun's core and the rate of loss of heat through the Sun's surface. This depends very much on the strength of the gravitational force. It is gravity that is responsible for capturing the material and for containing it. Were the gravitational force to be stronger, then everything would exert a stronger force on everything else. That in turn would mean we could get a temperature rise of a million degrees, and hence nuclear fusion, by compressing less hydrogen gas. Thus we would have had stars made up of less material, so there would be less fuel. Moreover, these smaller stars would leak heat more rapidly. This would have meant that the lifetime of stars would be reduced. We do not have to increase the strength of gravity by very much to find that there would be no stars living long enough for intelligent life to have evolved on a nearby planet. Increasing the strength of gravity by a factor of 2, for example, would increase the brightness of the Sun so much it would live for only 100 million years (instead of 10 billion).

That is but one hazard of having a stronger gravity. Another is that galaxies would be more compressed, with their constituent stars closer together – a similar situation to the one we encountered if the original "graininess" of the matter issuing from the big bang had been greater. The orbits of planets would be disturbed by close encounters with passing stars, thus affecting conditions on the planets – a consequence not conducive to the steady evolution of life.

Yet another effect of stronger gravity is that it would limit the type of life forms that could develop on a nearby planet. It would be more difficult to stand, and to move about in the enhanced attractive force of the planet's gravity. The complex life forms necessary for the development of intelligent life would involve so many atoms that such life forms might have difficulty withstanding the implosive force of their own gravity. For there to be any intelligent life within the universe, the force of gravity must not be too strong – and thankfully, it isn't.

We now have our rocky planet with the raw material needed for making the bodies of living creatures. The planet is in a stable orbit around a long-lived source of energy. Are there any further potential hazards to the development of life lying ahead?

What we do know is that to have life we need to be able to create very complex, organized molecular structures – those characteristic of biological entities. Here we come across something very strange but often overlooked: namely, *the self-organizing nature of matter*. What do we mean by that? Well, suppose you were yourself put in the position of having to create a universe. What would your basic building blocks look like? Small round spheres, much as we might imagine atoms to be – spheres capable of sticking together? If that were to be your choice, and you just allowed things to bang into each other, you would end up with nothing more than uninteresting shapeless blobs. Even if you replaced the spheres with tiny cubes, you would still end up with them sticking together in a haphazard fashion, resulting in a mess. But actual atoms are not like that. Their shapes, and the ways they bind to each other, are governed by quantum theory. We cannot go into that here; it all gets a little too complicated. It is sufficient for our purposes to note that the application of quantum theory results in there being set configurations for how a certain set of atoms can combine.

For example, when two atoms of hydrogen and one of oxygen combine to produce a water molecule, they do so according to a set pattern. The angle between the two bonds between each atom of hydrogen and that of oxygen is, in all cases, 104.45 degrees. It is because of such patterns that a complex molecule such as DNA is able to adopt its highly organized shape as a double helix. In contrast, it is so easy to imagine a world where the basic building blocks were of a kind that did not have such an intrinsic potentiality for producing interesting shapes – what we call the self-organizing nature of matter.

Mention of water does, of course, remind us of how indispensable water is for life. In seeking signs of life on other planets, such as Mars, one of the first questions to be addressed is the availability of water. As you will know, water has the odd property that when it solidifies (forms ice), contrary to what we might have expected, it expands, and as a result floats on liquid water. It has been speculated that this possibly made an important contribution to the evolutionary process, in that the ice forming on the surface of a pond or lake effectively insulates the water underneath from further severe heat loss. This in turn means that the lower levels remain liquid. In the past, that would have allowed primitive creatures down there to remain alive until more clement weather arrived.

So far we have taken it for granted that out of the big bang there came electrons, neutrons, and protons – particles possessing the properties they happen to have. But if there had been no electrons, there would have been no atoms. No neutrons would have meant there would have been no build-up of nuclei beyond hydrogen.

We have spoken of the potentially disastrous effects of changing the strengths of the nuclear and gravitational forces. What about the electric force? If the strength of the electric force had been stronger, the repulsion between protons would have been too great for them to combine to produce complex nuclei.

Then there is the simple observation that everything we see around us is made up of matter – matter as opposed to antimatter. For each type of fundamental particle (proton, neutron, electron, etc.) there is an antiparticle possessing the same mass, but having opposite values of other properties. For instance, whereas the proton has positive electric charge, its antiparticle will have negative electric charge. All this is well known, and antiparticles are readily produced in collisions of protons, say, in particle accelerators such as the Large Hadron Collider at the CERN laboratory in Geneva. When a particle meets up with its antiparticle they annihilate each other with the production of electromagnetic radiation, for example. It is expected that almost equal numbers of particles and their antiparticles came out of the big bang. In their subsequent collisions they disappeared, producing radiation that contributed the general cosmic background radiation. All except a small remnant. For some reason, the amount of matter coming out of the big bang slightly exceeded the amount of antimatter. Not very much: about one part in a billion. Once all the antimatter had been eliminated, we were left with the little bit of excess matter that makes up the universe we see today. Again, it is fortunate for us that there was that slight excess.

These then are some of the conditions that had to be satisfied in order for us to have put in our appearance. Let us summarize. They concerned:

- inflation to ensure against a premature big crunch;

- the accelerated expansion of the universe arising out of dark energy being unaccountably weak;

- the inherent "graininess" of matter at early times that led to the formation of galaxies and stars;

- the strength of the nuclear forces being neither too weak nor too strong;

- the fortuitous occurrence of the nuclear resonance that facilitated the formation of carbon;

- the three-dimensional nature of space giving rise to the inverse square law of gravitation and hence stable orbits for planets;

- the strength of the gravity force not being so strong as to significantly reduce the active lifetime of the Sun and other stars;

- the peculiar properties of water;

- the existence of electrons, protons, and neutrons;

- the electric force not being too strong;

- the slight excess of matter over antimatter.

Is the list definitive? Not really. Various authors have had different ways of getting across the same message. Is the list exhaustive? Might there be other features of the universe we are taking for granted, and perhaps ought not to? And note that all we have talked about so far derives from physics and cosmology. What about biology? Did it require some odd "coincidence" to allow the first cell to form, for instance? What about the first multicellular organism?

What all this adds up to is that, contrary to what we were saying at the beginning of this chapter about the universe being hostile to life (or at least what Steven Weinberg was saying), the cosmos has seemingly bent over backwards in innumerable ways to accommodate us. The universe is friendly to life. It appears to have been fine-tuned for life. This observation is known as *the Anthropic Principle*. This in turn raises the question: How are we to account for it?

In the first place, I suppose we must ask whether it was, in fact, all a matter of luck. This almost certainly cannot be right. It is hard, if not impossible, to put a figure on the odds of getting all the conditions right purely by chance. If the strength of the nuclear force, for instance, could theoretically have taken on any conceivable value, then the range of values we found that permit the development of life would be a small finite range divided by infinity, and the result would be zero. It is safe to say that the chances of all the conditions being right simply through random chance are smaller than that of winning the jackpot in the lottery – week, after week, after week…

If we are religious, the answer to the problem posed by the Anthropic Principle might appear obvious. The universe looks as though it has been fine-tuned for life because it *has* been fine-tuned for life. And the designer is God. We might be further tempted to add, "Therefore you must believe in God." However, going that extra step does remind us of an earlier argument for God's existence based on the notion of design: William Paley pointing to the way everything about the human body (like the watch found on the beach) is so beautifully fitted to fulfil its function it must have been consciously designed by Someone. We know what happened to that argument: along came Darwin's theory of evolution. So I would urge caution over any attempt to use the Anthropic Principle as an attempted *proof* of the existence of God – one aimed at convincing an atheist. But leaving that aside, the idea that God designed the universe primarily as a home for life is certainly one possibility.

Does science have anything to say on the subject? There are those who hold out the hope that one day a scientific theory will come along to show that the world is the way it is because that is the only way it could have been. There are no "coincidences"; there was no alternative. Personally I find it extremely difficult to see how that could come about. As we have noted, there are so many conditions that had to be satisfied. Moreover, they are of such a wide variety, it is hard to see how any theory could be so comprehensive and all-embracing as to account for all the disparate features involved.

But what if we are dealing with more than the one universe? How about the multiverse idea we came across in the last chapter? There we saw how a currently favoured theory, M-theory, suggests that our universe might not be alone. There could be many universes – perhaps an infinite number of them. Furthermore, the same theory indicates that all these universes are likely to have different laws of nature. Indeed, they could have their own space and time. Though the vast majority of those universes will have no life in them – because one or more of the conditions for life had not been satisfied – it would not be altogether surprising if one of them, or a few of them, purely by chance, happened to satisfy all the right conditions. We, being a form of life, were bound to find ourselves in one of these "freak" universes; we obviously couldn't have found ourselves in one of the others. Hence the problem is solved.

It appears to me that if we reject the idea of a Designer God, then the multiverse has to be the answer. This, I nevertheless hasten to add, is not to say that the multiverse idea is necessarily against belief in God. Certainly atheists are likely to *have* to accept it; for them there seems no alternative. But acceptance of a multiverse is also open to believers. Indeed, it might be argued that a God who used the process of evolution on Earth to create humans – together with lots of other varied and interesting creatures – might well be the kind of God who brought not only our universe into being, but also lots of other varied and interesting universes. Doubtless God would take a special interest in any universe, like ours, that gave rise to sentient beings that could relate to him. But God could also presumably enjoy and take an interest in all the other universes. This is in much the same vein as one imagines God taking a special interest in us humans, but also enjoying the other products of the evolutionary process on Earth.

Acceptance of the multiverse idea would be the ultimate step in placing our existence here on Earth in perspective. It was originally thought that the Earth was the centre around which everything rotated. It was discovered, however, that the Earth was just a planet – one among others orbiting the Sun. The Sun was just an ordinary star – one of 100 billion other stars belonging to the Milky Way galaxy. That galaxy, in turn, was but one of 100 billion galaxies belonging to the observable universe – that observable universe being part of the overall universe. Now we are faced with the possibility that our overall universe might be but one of an unimaginable number of other universes.

Making these discoveries has been a humbling experience. Some draw the conclusion that it all goes to show how insignificant and unimportant we individuals are. That is one interpretation. Another is to conclude that the awesome nature of the cosmos reveals to us the sheer power of God. And if such a powerful God takes a personal interest in each one of us, then that should be a sufficient indication that we have ultimate worth. Admittedly in purely physical terms we do not count. If you or I were to go out of existence, that would have no effect on the Sun. But if the Sun were to go out of existence... No, physically we are insignificant. But once we bring to mind the whole question of consciousness, that surely alters the situation. Recall the words of Blaise Pascal:

Man is the feeblest reed in existence, but he is a thinking reed... though the universe were to destroy him, man would know that he was dying. While the universe would know nothing of its own achievement.

*It is not in space I must seek my human dignity, but in the ordering of my thought... Through space the universe swallows me up like a speck; through thought, I grasp it...
(Pensées)*

Why is the universe friendly to life?

Was it deliberately designed like that,
or is it just part of a much larger
multiverse picture?

6 EXTRATERRESTRIAL INTELLIGENCE

– I think the universe is so vast that it would be self-centred to say that there aren't any other life-forms out there.

– If extraterrestrial life is discovered it'll prove that religion is unreliable because we would not be so sacred or important as we made ourselves out to be.

– I don't think that the discovery of aliens would have any impact on religious belief, because if God created our life he can create life anywhere within the universe and it doesn't make us any less significant.

– The discovery of extraterrestrial life would harm religion no more than the discovery of a new bacteria.

– If superior extraterrestrial life was found, this would show that humans aren't special – we're not the pinnacle of creation; we're just not that important.

– Humans are full of their own self-importance.

– ET might go in for genetically engineering babies
   to be more intelligent.

– I want to believe there's aliens and if an alien
   came down to me and said, "I'm smarter than
   you," I'd say, "OK mate. I agree with you –
   you're smarter than me, but I could also find you
   someone else on this Earth that's smarter
   than me…"

When thinking about the universe we cannot help but wonder
whether there is life out there. As far as our Solar System
is concerned – the planets circling our Sun – there might be
some very primitive forms of life. We should have the answer
to that quite soon as a result of planned space probes. But not
intelligent life. No, if extraterrestrial intelligence (ETI) exists
then we must search further afield; we must look to planets
going round other stars.

And there is no shortage of them. One of the fastest growing
developments in modern astronomy today is the location of these
extrasolar planets, or *exoplanets*, as they are called. How do we
go about finding them?

Directly observing them is not easy. The problem is that the
light a typical planet sends us is so faint compared to that given
out by its accompanying star. At the time of writing, only about
ten exoplanets have been seen by direct observation. Such
observations have been possible only because these planets have
been exceptionally large – several times bigger than Jupiter. Also
they have been hot, so allowing us to detect them through the
infrared radiation they are emitting rather than by the light of
the star they are reflecting. Such planets are not likely to be
homes for life. In order to see smaller, more hospitable planets,
attempts are currently being made to develop techniques for
blocking out the star's light, so allowing us to see those smaller

planets directly. In doing so, we might be able to detect changes in the colour of the planet over its yearly cycle that might indicate vegetation varying in response to changes of season. This would be an indication that at least certain forms of life might have taken hold there. But until that is done we have to rely on more indirect methods for locating exoplanets.

The first of these is to look for stars that "wobble". Though we think and talk about planets orbiting a star – the Earth going round the Sun, for instance – this is not quite correct. Both the planet and the star are orbiting a point lying between them called their *centre of mass*. With the Sun having so much more mass than the Earth, this point is very close to the Sun, so to all intents and purposes we think of the Earth as going round the Sun. But actually the Sun itself is also in orbit about that point. For a very much heavier planet, the centre of mass of the system would be further out from the star, and it becomes more obvious that both the planet and the star are in motion. If the planet were the same mass as the star then they would be orbiting a point midway between them. The fact that stars possessing planets will be in motion about their centre of mass means that if the plane of the orbit is in line with us, there will be times when the star is moving away from us, and other times when it is coming towards us in its orbit. This motion affects the characteristics of the light we receive from it. As the star moves away, the wavelength of the light it emits is stretched out (i.e. moves towards the red end of the spectrum). Later, when the star moves towards us, the wavelength gets squashed up (i.e. it is blue shifted). This effect is called a *Doppler shift*. We get the same kind of effect with sound waves: a police siren sounds high pitched when the car is approaching, and drops as the car passes and goes away. So the aim is to find stars that have a periodic change to the wavelengths of the light emitted. Very tiny variations can be measured, down to speed differences of 1 metre/second. This, so far, has been the most productive method for finding exoplanets.

A second method is called the transit method, and involves the planet eclipsing the star. Again, if we happen to lie in the plane of the rotation of the planet about its star, there will be times when the planet passes between the star and ourselves, so blocking a little of the star's light. So we look for stars the brightness of which dims for a while before being restored to its original level – a pattern of behaviour that is regularly repeated as the planet continues in the same orbit.

Sometimes, however, we find that the periodic dimming due to the transit of the planet is not exactly regular; the planet's orbit is being disturbed. Such perturbations arise from the presence of another planet belonging to the same star. The study of these variations in the transit times of one planet thus opens up a means for detecting the presence of the additional planet. This method is especially promising for the detection of Earth-sized planets.

A handful of exoplanets have been discovered by further techniques, but the methods described above have been the main ones. The early discoveries were made by ground-based telescopes. But with the launch in 2009 of the Kepler space telescope, the emphasis has switched to making observations from space where we do not encounter problems to do with looking through the Earth's atmosphere. As of 5 December 2011, the Kepler mission had identified 2,326 candidate exoplanets.

As a result of this work, we now know that at least 10 per cent of Sun-like stars are believed to have exoplanets. That means there are at least 50 billion exoplanets in our galaxy. Most of the planets so far discovered have been massive – similar to our Jupiter. This is because the detection techniques used have been biased towards big planets capable of producing significant stellar "wobbles", transit dimmings, etc. With increased sensitivity, it is expected that we shall soon be able to detect Earth-like planets. To date Kepler has found sixty-eight planets that are less than twice the size of the Earth, six of which lie in what is called the *habitable* zone – that is to say, the region about the star where it is expected that temperatures are in a range where there can be liquid water on the surface of the planet, and life could possibly flourish. On this basis the team estimate that 5.4 per cent of stars host Earth-like planets.

Summing this up, we find that there is no shortage of locations throughout the cosmos where intelligent life could take a hold. Which is not to say that it has. How can we find out whether there is ETI?

The obvious answer seems to be that we should get in a spacecraft and go and visit them, as is done in countless science fiction adventure stories. However, this is not a practicable proposition. The distances are just too vast. The alternative is to search the skies for signs that ETI is trying to communicate with us across space by sending us radio signals. Searches along these lines have been carried out by the Search for Extraterrestrial Intelligence (SETI) project for the past thirty years, but without success. So, for the time being at least, we are stuck; we have to try and guess what is the more likely answer.

There are many scientists who believe that, while primitive life forms might have started elsewhere, there were so many hurdles that had to be negotiated on the way to getting intelligent life here on Earth, it is quite possible that it has happened only the once. Out of the entire cosmos, we humans are the only ones to know it is there. If that were to be the case, then no new questions are raised for religion. There is no ETI.

However, I suspect that the majority of us, faced with the knowledge we now have of the mind-bogglingly vast number of different habitable locations there are in the universe, would expect that it is more likely that ETI does indeed exist. In which case, we should be considering how that prospect affects the way we ought to be viewing human life in the overall scheme of things, and in particular what sort of impact such knowledge has for religious belief.

First let us address the question of numbers. We cannot help but feel insignificant when faced with the prospect that the cosmos could be teeming with creatures at least as intelligent as ourselves. But is this anything new? We already recognize that as far as the conduct of life here on Earth is concerned, we as individuals have no real significance. Whatever you and I do is not likely to have much, if any, impact on the billions that make up the human race. Such significance as we have has always been confined to the impact we might have on the lives of those belonging to our circle of acquaintances – family, friends, neighbours, classmates, work colleagues, et al. In this context, the fact that there might be trillions of aliens out there, in addition to the billions of other humans on Earth, is irrelevant.

If we are religious, then we hold that we have significance in the eyes of God. This has always been a mystery. We ourselves can take a personal interest in no more than a handful of people. How can God take an intimate interest in each and every human being? For this to be the case, we have already had to accept that God must have some totally different way of relating to people than we do. That being so, God can presumably also take on board the aliens.

Much more important than mere numbers is the question of how our standing would be affected were we to find ETI to be vastly more intelligent than ourselves. As we have seen, evolution has taken a long time – several billion years – to produce us humans. *Homo sapiens* emerged about a million years ago. Around that time our ancestors had a brain weighing about 400 g; our brains today weigh 1.4 kg. The use of language – so important to the development of intelligence – became common only around 100,000 years ago. So we are relative newcomers onto the scene. That being the case, the evolution of ETI on some other planet had only to get out of step with what happened here on Earth to a comparatively small extent for them to have reached our stage of development a long time ago – millions and millions of years ago. Which, of course, raises the question as to what they would be like now.

In accord with the way our own development has been marked by an ever-increasing level of intelligence, our first guess might be that ETI would, by now, have an intelligence vastly superior to ours. They would regard us humans in much the same way as we regard a chimpanzee, or even a worm. But let us not jump to conclusions. We have developed this level of intelligence because having a superior intelligence had survival value for its owner. It meant having a better chance of surviving to the point where they could mate and pass on their higher intelligence to their offspring. The less intelligent had less chance of mating and passing on their inferior genes. Hence the next generation were, on average, slightly more intelligent than the previous one. And then the scene was set to repeat itself, leading to ever improved levels of intelligence. But is that still true today? Do we find that the more intelligent people have a greater chance of living to an age when they can marry and have children? That sounds most unlikely. If anything, I would have thought it was the other way round. The more intelligent you are, the better your chances of getting a well-paid job, and hence the higher your standard of living. But statistics show that the higher your standard of living, the *fewer* children you are likely to have. This sort of argument might lead us to deduce that, far from humans continuing to become more intelligent, we might now be in decline – a decline temporarily masked by better teaching in schools (or possibly grade inflation at GCSE, A level, and degree level(?!)). Perhaps the same has occurred with ETI. They got to our stage a long time ago, but have since made no further progress in this regard.

On the other hand, we need to bear in mind that if ETI reached our level, they probably knew all about genetics. They would have done the equivalent of our Human Genome Project and sequenced their DNA. They would then have been in a position to undertake genetic engineering. In particular, if they had so chosen, they could have genetically engineered designer babies to specification. They could have produced babies with desirable characteristics – greater intelligence, for example. From then on it would not have been a case of relying on the rather hit-and-miss process of evolution by natural selection. It would have been a case of what we might call *directed evolution*. We ourselves are approaching the point where this procedure becomes a practicable possibility. Indeed, we look forward to the time when we can identify those defective genes that lead to congenital disorders, such as sickle cell anaemia, and eliminate them from the gene pool so that they become a thing of the past. However, the idea of designer babies is another matter. The notion of selecting to have babies with specific characteristics (blond, blue-eyed, etc.) tends to fill us with revulsion. Would we ever countenance a situation where those judged to have less intelligence were sterilized, while future Einsteins lived in stud farms? Most unlikely. But that is not to say that ETI would necessarily feel bound by the same prohibitions. Perhaps they would see nothing wrong in going down that path. Indeed, they might see it as their duty to seize this opportunity of consciously and deliberately enhancing all desirable characteristics in order to promote the well-being of future generations, and to benefit their species.

Except that there is yet something further we must take into account. Having reached our stage of development, they would have learned not only about genetics, but also about nuclear power. Just like us, they would have been put in a position whereby they could destroy themselves. Those of us old enough to have lived through the cold war that followed on from World War II will recall the daily fear of living in the shadow of the bomb – the possibility of an imminent nuclear holocaust caused either by an act of war beginning with a pre-emptive strike, or by some false alarm triggered by a computer fault or human failing leading to a catastrophic misunderstanding between nations. With the ending of the cold war, this threat has seemed to recede. The *Doctor Strangelove* film no longer causes quite the chill in our hearts that it once did. But the threat has not gone away. How long will it be before some crazed fanatic takes control of a country with a nuclear capability? We trust that this is a distant prospect. But when talking about the development of a species through evolution, we are dealing with very long time spans. We must therefore ask what the odds might be that the human race can avoid all the potential triggers for a nuclear holocaust over, say, the next million years. I myself would not be all that confident.

And if that is true for us, might it not also be true of ETI? Like us, ETI would be a product of evolution by natural selection, with all that that implies regarding the imprinting into the DNA of behavioural characteristics such as aggression – behaviour conducive to the survival of their ancestors, but fatal when backed by a nuclear capability. Perhaps this is the fate of all intelligent creatures throughout the cosmos. They reach our level of intelligence, discover the Bomb, and within a comparatively short time (evolutionarily speaking) annihilate themselves. In which case, we might at least console ourselves with the thought that we humans are an example of the highest form of intelligence that ever develops in the universe.

Having said all that, however, let us set aside such gloomy thoughts and instead embrace the possibility that certain forms of ETI have indeed successfully avoided such a hazard, and somehow or other (perhaps through designer babies) have achieved a level of intelligence that is vastly superior to our own. What would the significance of that be, especially for religious thought?

It is customary to think that God takes a greater interest in us humans than he does in the other animals on Earth. Unlike them, we are able to relate to God. It requires intelligence to recognize the possible existence of God and what kind of god we are dealing with. We are able to enter into a loving relationship with him. This is held to be of overwhelming significance in that God's most important characteristic is love. Love is what it is all about. For Christians, the eternal Son of God took on human form; he did not come as one of the other animals. There would have been no point in him doing that. Without language and the ability to communicate widely, such an incarnation would have passed largely unrecognized. We sometimes hear it asked why Jesus lived at the particular time he did. It can be argued that it was probably the earliest time when there was a good chance of knowledge of that event being spread worldwide – through the outreach of the Roman Empire.

So if we are right in deducing that God does indeed take a greater interest in us than the other animals, largely as a result of us having a superior intelligence, does it not follow that God would place an even higher value on a superior form of ETI? Would that not mean that critics of religion are correct in claiming that religious people have an over-inflated assessment of the importance of humans in the overall scheme of things?

Before jumping to that conclusion, we need to take into account that nowhere in religious thinking is a high premium placed on intelligence for its own sake. Certainly, as we have stated, a basic level of intelligence is required in order to recognize that there is a god with whom we can relate. But beyond that, there is no reason to think that God has a greater interest in those with an above average IQ. As we have said, what matters is the degree of our love for God and for our fellow human beings. This is made abundantly clear in Christ's two great commandments: "You shall love the Lord your God with all your heart, and with all your soul, and with all your mind, and with all your strength" and "You shall love your neighbour as yourself". We all know of exceedingly clever people who, being wholly bound up in seeking celebrity, money, and power, appear to lack a spiritual dimension to their lives. While, on the other hand, there are those who are intellectually challenged but are nevertheless blessed with deep spiritual insights. In this regard, we would do well to recall how Jesus chose Peter, a humble fisherman with little in the way of intellectual gifts, to be the rock on which the church was to be founded. Such considerations seem to suggest that even if ETI were superior to us in intelligence, that would not necessarily imply that God had a greater interest in them than in us.

If, as we have said, love is what it is all about, then we need further to recall something else Jesus said: "Greater love has no one than this, that he lay down his life for his friends" (John 15:13). History is full of examples of martyrs who have laid down their lives for God and for their fellows. This is the ultimate sacrifice; as proof of love, it cannot be bettered. So in what way could a superior form of ETI demonstrate a closer bond with God, and as a consequence, be more highly valued by God?

This is not to say that ETI would be incapable of having a deeper spiritual awareness of God and of God's love for them. We know that humans experience God in very different ways. For some, it is given for them to enjoy ecstatic mystical experiences. Others might encounter uplifting moments when confronted with the beauty of nature, or the awe-inspiring contemplation of the heavens. For yet others, religion is a more pragmatic affair of just loyally soldiering on doing what they believe to be the will of God. Who is to know what experiences of the Divine might come with the superior capabilities of an advanced form of ETI? Just as we suspect that we have a richer spiritual awareness of God than our primitive ancestors did in the past, or indeed dolphins and chimpanzees might have today, so might ETI have a more highly developed sensitivity to the spiritual. But that does not necessarily mean God has to take a greater interest in them. In which case, the discovery of ETI would not have the devastating impact on religion that some prophesy.

Except that, for Christians at least, there is one further topic that needs to be addressed. Central to the Christian conception of our relationship with God is the part played by the life, death, and resurrection of Jesus. It is held that he died to save us from our sins. But what possible significance could this have for ETI? It all took place on planet Earth. ETI would know nothing about it. Are we to understand that the eternal Son of God, having taken on human form for our sake, would have undergone further incarnations, appearing in the form of ETI on other planets? That would certainly be one possibility. It can be argued that ETI, being a product of the evolutionary struggle, would probably have inherited genetically influenced behaviour patterns orienting them, to some extent, towards selfishness and aggression. In which case they might well need a saviour like us – one prepared to sacrifice himself for them.

But before jumping to that conclusion, we need to take a closer look at this whole question of sacrifice. As the appropriate entry in the *Oxford Companion to Christian Thought* puts it: "Sacrifice is one of the most inescapable, impenetrable, and off-putting themes in Christian thought... it has provoked serious divisions between churches and proved repellent to many sensitive Christians." It is indeed inescapable. Jesus is constantly referred to as the Lamb of God. There are no fewer than 213 references to sacrifice in the Bible. And it is not difficult to see why the subject is so controversial. How does punishing an innocent animal, or in the case of Christ an innocent man, make matters right? On the contrary, we might think it makes matters *worse*. Under normal circumstances we would call this a gross miscarriage of justice.

The practice of sacrifice goes back to ancient times when people believed in many gods. These gods were in charge of certain territories, and they looked after and protected the people who lived there. They were warlike, fighting gods. The people in their turn had to look after their god. They had to feed them. This they did by burning sacrifices. The flames and the smoke went up to the gods and fed them. There was also in this the idea that life comes out of death. The seed dies and gives life to the new plant. The animal dies and that enhances the life of the god. Life is also associated with blood. If you lose a lot of blood you lose your life. So an excess of blood on the god's altar gives the god life.

There then grew up the idea of the gods being angry when the people did wrong. How to make amends? How to placate them? Sacrifice what is precious to you. A first-born lamb, for example. The people were poor. It was a terrible wrench to give up one of their prized possessions – a lamb; they might not be left with enough to eat themselves. So, not only was the lamb itself suffering for their sins (it was otherwise going to be slaughtered for food at a later date anyway), but they themselves were also paying the price for what they had done.

But then over the course of time there appeared the idea that there was just the one God and that he was a God of love and mercy and forgiveness. Dissident voices were heard. Psalm 51, for example, declares: "For thou desirest not sacrifice; else would I give it: thou delightest not in burnt offering. The sacrifices of God are a broken spirit: a broken and a contrite heart, O God, thou wilt not despise" (16–17).

However, the practice continued. It was still going on at the time of Jesus. So, one way of viewing Jesus' sacrifice of himself was to put a stop to it once and for all. By sacrificing himself in place of a lowly animal – the perfect human being and the Son of God himself – this ultimate sacrifice was so stupendous as to render all others worthless. And, indeed, in time the practice of sacrifice through the slaughter of animals came to an end. This then is one approach to the subject of sacrifice, and particularly the sacrifice of our Lord. It is a rather negative approach. It is putting a stop to a practice that God did not want anyway. That being so, we might argue that if ETI had never taken up the idea of making such sacrifices in the first place, there would be no need for the Son of God to go to them to put a stop to it.

But then there is a wholly different way of looking at the subject – a positive way. We have said how eventually the god of the ancient Jews – the warlike, tribal god of the Jews – was replaced by the universal God of all peoples. Moreover, it came to be recognized that the defining characteristic of God is that he is a God of love. How do we *demonstrate* our love for another person? We have already noted that it is not through having good times together, but from how we put ourselves out for the other person. How much we sacrifice our own interests for them. As was mentioned just now, Christ said that greater love can no man have than to lay down his life for his friends. This is the ultimate sacrifice, and the clinching proof of love. That is what God wants from us: if necessary we are to go as far as laying down our lives for the other person as the perfect expression of love.

But does this not raise a problem for God himself? God himself is perfect love. It is not sufficient for him to merely offer us advice as to how he wants *us* to behave – or indeed for him to be very caring, and loving, and helpful, and friendly towards us. For him to demonstrate the greatest love anyone can have, God too must pay the absolute price. He must be prepared to lay down his life for us. If he does not – if he just shouts encouragement to us from the sidelines – then we lowly humans can outdo God himself by laying down our lives for another in a way that he is *not* called upon to do. So what we see on the cross is not a man offering his life to an angry god demanding recompense. This is God himself laying down his life for us. It is not even God demonstrating what he wants us to do (though it is, of course, such a demonstration); that is not the main point. God feels himself *compelled* to go through with this act because this is the only way he can give expression to his perfect love. Even if we were not sinful, he would probably still have done it. He would not have been able to help himself. His perfect love had to find its perfect expression. And paying the ultimate sacrifice was the only way of doing it.

If this is indeed a valid way of interpreting Christ's action on the cross, then this would seem to imply that God would also want to express his love for ETI in the same way. That in turn argues for further incarnations in the form of ETI.

So much for the death of Christ. What about his resurrection and his subsequent appearances to the disciples and other followers? Integral to Christian belief, and that of other religions, is the idea of life beyond death. But what indications are there that there is such a dimension to life? The overwhelming argument for Christians is that Christ himself demonstrated its reality through his own resurrection. That being so, it could be argued that it would not be right for us humans to have the advantage of such a demonstration, and not ETI. Again we have a reason for believing in further incarnations.

But, arguing in the opposite sense, we might also point out that there have been many humans who did not have the advantage of knowing about the life, death, and resurrection of Jesus: all those who lived before the time of Christ. The great figures of the past – Abraham, Moses, Elijah, and all the other God-fearing people of those times – showed that one could come into a relationship with God without a personal knowledge of Jesus. The same goes for the faithful adherents to the other great world religions seeking God by different paths today. Though they might have heard of Jesus, it is perhaps unfair to expect them to go against their culture and upbringing and switch to Christianity if they have already found God by an alternative route. God must therefore have some way of dealing with those for whom Christ is not an acknowledged force in their lives. That being the case, perhaps God would have something else in mind for ETI that would not involve them having their own form of saviour.

Bearing all this in mind, it is up to each of us to reach our own conclusions about how ETI might relate to God.

What impact would the discovery of extraterrestrial intelligence have on religion?

In general, how would such a discovery alter your assessment of the importance, or otherwise, of us humans?

7 PSYCHOLOGY

— Sigmund Freud showed that religion is based on believing things to be true – that you believe them to be true because you want them to be true.

— Freud believed that when we're younger we have a father figure and he protects us when we're vulnerable. As we grow older we're still vulnerable and therefore we come up with some heavenly father who protects us – and I think that's what religious believers do.

— Freud dismisses religion as being illogical and you know having a lack of proof. But he's being very hypocritical because his own ideas, you know, they're based firmly on his interpretation, opinion and a confirmatory bias.

— People use religion as a way to comfort themselves, to get through life.

— I don't feel religion's just something made up because it's a comfort, because at many times it can mean being persecuted as well.

— The brain's a tangible object and it exists in the physical world, so it's governed by the laws of nature so free will's just an illusion.

– To say we have no free will is unrealistic. I think
   that in every day we have a choice to make.

– Just because our actions are predictable
   doesn't mean we have no free will. Just
   because someone says "I bet she'll choose that
   top" doesn't mean she didn't choose.

Sigmund Freud, the father of psychology, was strongly opposed
to religion:

> *Religion is comparable to a childhood neurosis... The whole*
> *thing is so patently infantile, so foreign to reality.*
> (New Introductory Lectures on Psychoanalysis, *1933)*

What were his grounds for being so dismissive? He held that,
as a child, we start out feeling helpless. We look to our earthly
parents for comfort and protection. On growing up, we continue
to wish for that kind of protection, and through what Freud
called *wish-fulfilment* we comfort ourselves by believing we have
an imaginary heavenly father figure. Religion is thus to be seen
as a childish delusion. Atheism, on the other hand, confronts
these fears and deals with them in a mature, grown-up manner.

There is undoubtedly *something* to this line of reasoning.
Surveys reveal that among those who believe in God, the *kind*
of God we believe in is very much coloured by the kind of earthly
father we have had. If he was a strict disciplinarian, then God is
seen to be a strict disciplinarian. And the opposite is true; if your
earthly father was more easy-going, then that is how you see
God. So clearly we are, to some extent, projecting characteristics
onto God. But whether the whole thing is a projection is another
matter.

Freud saw religion as a comfort. And there is a certain amount
of truth in that too. It *is* comforting to think that there might be

a life beyond death, say. Religious believers generally belong to a community of like-minded people. Through the church, mosque, temple, or synagogue we can turn to others for sympathetic help in times of trouble. But leading a religious life can also be far from comforting. We are called upon to make sacrifices – having to get up in the morning to attend acts of worship, fasting, giving heavily to charity, not having sex outside marriage. There might even be situations where we have to give up our life for the cause. As we have noted, history records many martyrs who have felt compelled to make the ultimate sacrifice.

Freud being such a dominant figure in the development of psychology, and his views on religion being so well known, there has been a tendency among the general public for the impression to be gained that the study of psychology inevitably leads to atheistic conclusions: psychology has explained away religion. Moreover, Freud regarded psychology as a science, to rank alongside the physical sciences. Accordingly, this was yet another example of science catching out religion.

The grounds for claiming psychology to be a science rest on the idea that it consists of conclusions based on observations – the observations made on patients. That is true. However, it is a big step to go from an account of someone's dreams, for example, to an interpretation as to what they might mean. In making such interpretations, Freud was given to making *ex cathedra* pronouncements that appear to many to be very hard to substantiate. Not only that, but his observations could hardly be thought of as being based on an unbiased sample of the population, dealing as he did predominantly with patients who had severe psychiatric disorders.

Another of the prominent founder figures of psychology was Carl Jung. For a while he worked with Freud. But in time he found Freud's conclusions so arbitrary that he went his own way. Jung had a completely different approach. Whereas Freud concentrated mostly on the early years of life and how childhood neuroses could have deleterious knock-on effects later, Jung was more interested in the later stages of life and how one was eventually to achieve one's full potential. He noted that due to the pressures we are subject to – the demands made on us by our work, our family obligations, and so on – we develop only a fraction of our potential. At school and college, for instance, we are confronted at various stages with decisions as to which subjects we should study and which we should drop. And sometimes this can be a toss-up between two almost equally attractive options. Later, in order to succeed in the work place, we must concentrate on some narrow field of expertise. In so doing we neglect other potential skills we possess and could alternatively have honed. Jung held that the aim of the later stages of life was to go some way towards correcting these biases whereby only certain of one's abilities had been given the opportunity to flourish, the others being neglected. One needed to make good those aspects of one's personality that so far had not been allowed to come to fruition. This process of creating a well-rounded personality was given the name *individuation*. And we can see this process being successfully pursued by many people who, when they retire from full-time employment, engage in all sorts of activities they had not previously had time for, such as art, travel, gardening, or a whole range of other hobbies and activities.

Jung then went on to declare that just as every rounded object, such as a ball, has to have a centre, a well-rounded personality also has to have a centre. And for Jung that centre was the God-image within us. So, what is this "God-image"?

Jung took the concept of the unconscious mind developed by Freud, and expanded on it. According to his theory of the mind, in addition to having a *personal unconscious*, harbouring such things as memories of previous experiences, we also have what he called the *collective unconscious*. This is something we have in common. We are born already possessing certain attitudes of mind – what he called *archetypes*. These lead us to have elemental tendencies to behave instinctively in particular ways. Archetypes are organizing principles. They might be likened to jelly moulds. In themselves they are empty. But they shape and form one's actual experiences. The word "archetype" means "imprint". There are, for example, "mother" and "father" archetypes, which predispose us to act in certain ways towards our parents. There is the "wise old man" archetype, which inclines us to accept the authority of certain individuals, and a "hero" archetype, which orientates us to follow a charismatic leader, perhaps with blind allegiance. These and others Jung identified through a variety of sources, including a study of recurring themes to be found in ancient and enduring myths that have resonated with people down the ages. There is clearly some connection between these archetypes and the genetically influenced behaviour patterns we spoke of in our discussion of evolution. Such behaviour patterns and archetypes we all have in common, and are ours from the moment of conception.

Jung claimed the God-image to be one of these archetypes, and that it has especial significance. For him religion, far from being a childish illusion, was at the very core of being a wholesome mature person. He once wrote:

> *Among all my patients in the second half of life – that is to say, over 35... it is safe to say that every one of them fell ill because he had lost that which living religions of every age have given to their followers...*
> (Modern Man in Search of a Soul, *1933)*

The process of individuation is one where you find your true self as an individual. This uncovering of the real you confronts you with the God-image lying at the very core of your being. Getting to know yourself is irrevocably bound up with sorting out your relationship with God. The God-image is indeed sometimes called the Self – hence its position at the very centre of the psyche – the psyche being the sum total of one's mental capacity, conscious and unconscious.

Closely related to all this is the notion that everyone has within them a religious drive. By this one means we have an inborn tendency to devote ourselves to a cause. This does not necessarily orient us towards God. The object of our zeal might be animal rights, a political party, Green issues, a street gang, a football club, etc. I well recall a small gathering of scientists and psychologists I attended at St George's House, Windsor. It was a meeting convened by Prince Philip to discuss science and religion. The opening speaker on the first evening was someone I did not know at the time: Peter Atkins of Oxford University. He gave this talk which was a paean of praise extolling the wonders of science. Science was all-powerful; it would one day know the answers to all questions; it was awesome; there was no greater calling than to be a scientist. I must confess that although I myself love science, I felt Atkins was rather overdoing it! Then the penny dropped. I realized that every time he spoke of science, we could substitute the word "God". He was setting us up; it was a spoof. However, as the talk progressed, I began to wonder when he planned to come clean and reveal that it was all an Aunt Sally – an ingenious way to stir up the subsequent debate. But then he sat down. That was it. To the astonishment of myself, and others present, it dawned on us that it was not a joke; he actually meant every word he had said. The following morning over breakfast, the Jungian psychologists had a field day analysing him on the basis of what he had said. Science had become his god.

Jung held that the object of our religious drive *ought* to be God, and these others were substitutes for that. The existence of this God-image was not in itself to be regarded as proof of the existence of an objective God. That for Jung was not part of psychology. The study of psychology should limit itself to the observation that, for whatever reason, we do have this God-image within us, and that it is central to our well-being. In point of fact, in his personal life, Jung did believe in God. Actually that is not quite right. He once gave a famous TV interview in which he was asked whether he believed in God. He replied: "I know. I don't need to believe. I know."

So, through those founder figures of psychology, Freud and Jung, we have two very contrasting views as to the place of religion in the life of the mature person.

One of today's severest and best-known critics of religion is the biologist Richard Dawkins. He has introduced the term "meme". A meme is an idea, or set of ideas, that spreads through society from one person to another – parents passing it on to their children, for example. Bad or harmful memes he likens to a virus. As with a flu virus, it spreads and infects otherwise healthy minds. Religion he regards as one of these harmful viruses. He is all for eliminating it and restoring people to their right minds again. It is an arresting idea. Dawkins can be a very persuasive advocate.

But cannot the whole idea be turned on its head? After all, anthropologists reliably inform us that most, if not all, ancient civilizations show signs of having been religious. It shows up, for instance, in the way they bury their dead – with its indications of a belief in an afterlife. This accords well with Jung's notion of there being a religious drive in us all. Occasionally there have been reports of isolated non-religious tribes. But when these claims have been reinvestigated, they have not been confirmed. Thus, we can argue that the *natural* state for humans is to be religious. What is *new* is this recent idea of atheism. It is atheism that is spreading. We see this, for example, in the decline of church attendance. So we are bound to ask which is the virus that is infecting the *natural* state of the mind. Is it religion, as Dawkins maintains, or atheism?

A currently favoured argument is that the religious drive has arisen because it has survival value. Banding together as a religious community enhanced our ancestors' chances of surviving to the point where they could mate and pass on their genes. It did not matter what they had in common; belief in an imaginary God would do as well as any other focus of shared loyalty. The important thing was that it led to individuals working together for their mutual benefit. Thus, according to this view, religion with its belief in God is just an artefact thrown up by the evolutionary process. In its day, it was a useful fiction.

There is no doubt that there are evolutionary advantages in being cooperative, in appropriate circumstances, rather than trying to go it alone. We came across this earlier in examining various forms of genetically influenced behaviour patterns. Theoretically, a belief in an imaginary God could be the cement holding a particular group of individuals together. The trouble with this idea, however, is that this focus for loyalty – an invisible God – is so tenuous. Even some of the most ardent religious believers can have a crisis of faith when they are plagued with doubts as to the reality of God. We would think that a group would have a better chance of sticking together if they had a common cause that was more tangible – something that clearly did exist: our family, following a charismatic leader, defending our neighbourhood, country, or race, and so on. These do indeed act as foci creating communities of people that act together.

A further objection to the idea of there being survival value for a community bound by belief in an imaginary God arises when we consider the supposed nature of this God, and the behaviour he demands from his followers. As we saw when considering whether there was likely to be survival value for an individual in being religious, it is hard to see why a predisposition to love our enemies and turn the other cheek was conducive to surviving to the point where we could mate and pass on such a tendency. Would a community that adopted such a passive attitude have survived in an environment where there were more self-centred and aggressive tribes?

Finally there is the question of *free will*. Our capacity to choose what course of action we should undertake is integral to religious belief. We are required to choose freely whether to follow Christ, for example. And what's more, we are to be held responsible for our chosen actions; we either gain eternal life or are consigned to the other place. So the question of whether we do actually have free will looms large in religious discussion.

Claims are made, on the basis of science, that free will is actually an illusion. Is that true? Our *mental* experience is that we are constantly having to make choices – choices that determine which of several possibilities will actually happen. But we do our thinking with our brain, and the brain is a physical object, and physical objects are subject to the laws of nature. We say the workings of the brain are *deterministic*. This raises an obvious problem. For example, at the present moment you are facing a choice. You can either carry on reading this, or alternatively you can lay the book aside and go and make a cup of tea. OK, you have decided to carry on reading – for the time being at least. Nevertheless, you could have chosen otherwise. Or could you? Suppose a scientist had carried out a thorough examination of all the contents of your brain immediately before you made your decision. She knows everything about its physical state at that point in time. Applying the laws of physics, she could presumably work out what the future state of your brain was going to be at some later instant – say at a time after you had made the decision. The first physical state corresponds to the mental state of being undecided; the second to the mental state of having made the decision. Does that not mean she could have predicted, not only what the future physical state of the brain was going to be, but also the mental state that went with it? Could she not therefore have predicted what your so-called "decision" was going to be? You had no freedom to act otherwise. It was all determined in advance. This is known as the *free will/determinism problem*: how to reconcile the grinding predictability of the physical brain with the mental sense that the future is open and depends on our choice.

One attempt at a solution is to invoke quantum theory. This is the theory that physicists have to use when describing the behaviour of very small objects such as atoms and electrons. Such constituent particles behave very differently from macroscopic objects like balls, chairs, cars, etc. Their behaviour is inherently unpredictable. It is embodied in something called the *uncertainty principle*. This holds that if you know precisely where a particle is located, you cannot at the same time know anything about its motion. Conversely, if you know all about how it is moving, you cannot at the same time know where it is positioned. But in order to predict its future, you need to know precisely where it is to begin with, *and* how it is moving. Thus its future behaviour *cannot* be determined. We are able to work out the odds on it ending up in any of a number of possible future states, but not exactly which one it will be. The actual outcome depends on chance. The reason we speak of the behaviour of large everyday objects, such as balls, as being determined is that they are made up of a vast number of these constituent atomic particles – to the extent that their individual random uncertainties average out. To within the limits of measurement precision customarily available when predicting the future behaviour of macroscopic objects, the behaviour appears, to all intents and purposes, to be deterministic.

The fact that behaviour is not strictly deterministic raises the possibility that quantum theory might hold the key to solving the free will/determinism problem. What if the key activity in the brain, leading to the making of a mental decision, lies at the atomic level, rather than at the level of a complex, larger biological entity? Suppose it depends on the behaviour of an individual atom, or even that of a subatomic particle. Under such circumstances, an inquisitive scientist examining the contents of the brain would *not* be able to determine what the future state of the brain was going to be at the level necessary for predicting the outcome of a "decision". As far as the scientist is concerned, the future remains open to various possibilities. All she can do is offer odds on a variety of potential outcomes.

This loosening of the deterministic chain of events can sound promising for those concerned to preserve the notion of free will. But wait. What have we replaced strict determinism with? Free conscious choice? No. It has been replaced by chance – random chance. Consider: If you cannot make up your mind on an issue, what can you do? Spin a coin: heads or tails. But is that you making a choice? No, that is you opting out of making a choice and instead leaving it to chance. Thus we are faced with a situation where a mental decision is made either at the atomic or subatomic level, in which case it is a manifestation of pure random chance, or at the aforementioned macroscopic level of the brain, in which case it is to all intents and purposes subject to determinism. Either way, it does not appear to be consonant with our idea of having free will.

The mind/body dualist approach to the problem, advocated by René Descartes, holds that the mind and body are separate entities that can interact with each other. The mind can act upon the brain causing it to change direction. That might be regarded as a commonsense way of preserving our untrammelled free will. The approach was contested by Gilbert Ryle in his book *The Concept of Mind*, where he dismissed it as "the ghost in the machine". This he did on the grounds that it was difficult to see how an immaterial mind could affect the material brain. What was the nature of the supposed force that was being applied to make the brain change course?

A modern-day version of this involves, once again, invoking quantum uncertainty. The idea is that decisions are made at the atomic level of the brain, and the mind works upon the uncertainties manifest at that level. The mind subtly changes the odds on the various possible outcomes in order to achieve its chosen end. It does this within the limits allowed by the uncertainty principle, so no law of physics is being violated. An imaginary scientist examining the brain would see nothing amiss. No new physical force is being applied. The mind is instead bringing its influence to bear on the mathematical odds.

Leaving this possibility aside, the purely mechanistic interpretation of the workings of the brain, based on determinism, appeared recently to have received a boost from the research work of Benjamin Libet and his co-workers. Subjects had electrodes fitted to their heads to monitor neuronal activity in the cortex. They were asked to perform some simple task such as pressing a button, or flexing a finger or wrist. This they were to do at a time of their own choosing. They did this sitting at a desk on which there was a monitor displaying a form of clock. Participants were asked to note the time when they were first aware that they were about to perform the act. This typically occurred 200 milliseconds before the equipment registered that the button, or whatever, had indeed been activated. Such a slight delay was only to be expected. What was surprising was that the equipment registered brain activity associated with the decision a full 500 milliseconds before the button was pressed. In other words, the information about the decision was there in the brain 300 milliseconds before the conscious mind became aware that the decision had indeed been taken. This experiment was carried out in 1983. Since 2008, further experimentation has revealed instances where the upcoming outcome of a decision could be found seven seconds before the act was committed.

So, what are we supposed to infer from this regarding whether we have free will or not? Some conclude that this is the final nail in the coffin. The so-called "decision" is actually being made in the material brain, and consciousness is merely giving voice to what has already been decided for it. We are therefore not responsible for making any choices.

But is that fair? If these experimental findings are confirmed, they will certainly show that we do not make our decisions consciously. But, as we have seen, there is more to the psyche than mere consciousness; there is the unconscious, both the personal unconscious, and what Jung called the collective unconscious. What is the *real* mental person? Is it what we happen to be consciously aware of at the present moment? Or is it more to do with the unconscious – that vast repository of memories, archetypes, and subconscious activity. The Libet experiment seems to be showing that our decisions are being made in the unconscious. But is that so surprising? The unconscious is not just a passive library of memories. It can intrude into consciousness by, for example, the making of Freudian slips, and the taking of actions which only later one might recognize as having some unconscious motivation. We all experience embarrassing situations where we cannot remember someone's name. No matter how hard we consciously try, it just will not come. So we get on with some other activity, only to find at some later point in time the name pops up. How? It seems as though, while we were consciously engaged elsewhere, the unconscious was busily searching through the files of the mind to find the missing name and so have it to hand when consciousness once again turned to the question. Then there are dreams. We do not consciously decide the content of our dreams (more's the pity!). It is something thrust into our conscious awareness by the unconscious wishing to give expression to its fears and other preoccupations. So the unconscious is a dynamic entity, and can reasonably claim to be a stronger candidate for being the true mental self than mere transitory awareness. According to such a perspective, the real mental you is indeed participating in the act of making a decision – one associated with the early brain activity investigated by Libet and his co-workers.

But might not all this discussion be founded on a misunderstanding as to what we mean by the term "free will"?

A dictionary definition states that it is the ability to choose. To choose what? To choose to do what we want to do. This, of course, is subject to external constraints of various kinds such as being disabled, or operating under the threat of punishment, as well as internal constraints arising from phobias such as a fear of heights. These constraints effectively limit the number of options from which we can choose. But among the feasible options, we do what we want. And this is what we find to be the case. We do act according to our wishes. We do not find ourselves deciding to act one way, only to discover that there is some inner unknown compulsion driving us helplessly to act differently. From this we conclude that we do indeed have free will, as so defined.

But does that rule out determinism at the brain level? Not necessarily. Why shouldn't the will, as so manifest, be at all times in tune with what the physical brain, following the dictates of the laws of physics, would in any case be doing? This is the *compatibilist argument*. It is an argument that claims that there is no either/or dilemma. Free will and determinism both apply.

A counter-argument to this is to take issue over the definition of free will that we have been using. The claim is that free will is not so much the ability to act as we choose, but the ability to act *otherwise*. But does that make sense? If we decided to act otherwise, we would, under those circumstances, still find ourselves acting according to our wish so to act. This alternative action would still have been the one you chose. So we are back to the original definition of free will. This is not to say that people don't from time to time act unpredictably. We say that someone "acted out of character". But what do we mean by that? Have they really gone against their true character and nature? Or is it more likely that they are of a contrarian nature and have deliberately decided, on this particular occasion, to act in a manner no one expects of them, perhaps in order to emphasize their independence? Again they have acted as they chose to act.

Summing up, we appear to face various possibilities. First, there is no such thing as free will; instead we are but helpless robots going through the motions on a tide of determinism. There is the "ghost in the machine" possibility: an immaterial mind acting on the brain, possibly by manipulating quantum uncertainties. Then there is the compatibility argument, which accepts determinism but claims that this does not invalidate the idea of free will: they are two sides of the same coin. Finally, I suppose we ought to add the possibility that when matter is arranged in the highly organized manner we find in the brain, the ordinary laws of nature are inadequate to explain all that is going on. Perhaps our familiar laws only strictly apply to simple systems, and some as yet unknown more far-reaching law is required to deal with the complexity found uniquely in the brain. Our familiar laws are in effect just approximations of that law – approximations adequate enough for the simple systems we observe, and experiment on, in the laboratory, but not for understanding the brain.

So what relevance does all this have for religion? As we have noted, it is a key feature of religious thinking that we are free to choose – to choose whether to enter into a loving relationship with God or not. And, having chosen, to be held responsible for that action and so reap the consequences.

In the absence of determinism, there is no problem. We have free will of a kind we are used to thinking of. Nothing is changed. But what if determinism holds? Even if we subscribe to the compatibility argument, it would appear that, because of the deterministic behaviour of the brain, the future is fixed; what will be, will be, regardless. How then can we be held *responsible* for our actions if we really had no alternative but to "choose" as we did? This is undoubtedly a big problem for believers.

I myself don't have an answer. All I can do is point out that this matter of free will in religion is much more complicated than generally thought. For example, what are we to make of the Old

Testament account of God informing Jeremiah: "Before you were born I set you apart; I appointed you as a prophet" (1:5)? Note: Before he was born. Jeremiah's future as a great prophet had already been mapped out for him. Then we have Jesus telling his disciples, "You did not choose me, but I chose you" (John 15:16). We read in the opening chapter of the book of Malachi that although Esau and Jacob were brothers, God declared, "Yet I have loved Jacob, but Esau I have hated" (1:2–3). Poor Esau! The odds seem to have been stacked against him from the start. In the first chapter of Paul's letter to the Ephesians he states: "For he chose us in him before the creation of the world to be holy and blameless in his sight. In love he predestined us to be adopted as his children through Jesus Christ, in accordance with his pleasure and will" (1:4–5) The same theme is taken up again in his letter to the Romans (8:29): "For those God foreknew he also predestined to be conformed to the likeness of his Son."

Predestination seems to imply God has already determined our future. And not only us as individuals. He elected the Jews to be his chosen people. Why the Jews rather than some other nation? They did not volunteer to be the people from whom the Messiah was to come. It was a role thrust upon them.

In addition to being expounded by Paul, predestination was strongly advocated by St Augustine. The Roman Catholic Church never taught it as official dogma, but the idea was revived at the Reformation and is particularly associated with Calvin. The doctrine remains controversial. It is not difficult to see why. Echoing the general philosophical free will/ determinism problem, it seems hard to reconcile the apparently conflicting notions of, on the one hand, having to make a free choice as to whether to love and serve God, and, on the other, bowing to an inevitable future role that has already been laid down by God. It also strikes us as unfair that some people, from the beginning of time, have been elected for salvation, while others stand condemned.

What grounds do we have today for giving credence to predestination? Well, it can sometimes seem strange that two people, possibly close brothers or sisters, with more or less the exact same family background and upbringing, can react to religion so differently. One will enter a church and immediately feel an affinity with the place – it is like a second home – while for the other it is altogether an alien environment. From time to time, it does appear that God especially puts his finger on some people and not others. We hear of people receiving a call from God to perform some special service. The call might not be as dramatic as that which Paul received on the road to Damascus, but can in its own way be as compelling. And there are those who, looking back over the course of their life, claim in retrospect to see a meaningful pattern. Incidents, which at the time seemed to make no sense, do with the benefit of hindsight appear after all to have been for the best. One discerns God's guiding hand at work. That, in any event, is the claim that is made. It is why the idea of predestination cannot be dismissed out of hand.

In addressing this subject, we need to draw a distinction between predestination and God's foreknowledge. The latter, as we have already noted, simply means that God outside of time is able to know the future. That in itself does not necessarily compromise our free choice, in the same way as we cannot argue that just because a wife knows that, come Saturday evening, her husband will be in front of the TV watching *Match of the Day*, means he is not exercising free will. She knows he will be choosing to do that because she knows him so well. God's knowing is like that – only even more certain. Predestination, however, goes further. It involves not only God knowing what we shall do, but actually having a hand in determining what that future action will be. It is that which seems to compromise our free will.

One approach to a resolution is to say that God has a plan for the world, and each of us has been assigned a part to play in its fulfilment. In other words, each of us has a planned destiny.

However, it is up to us to use our free will to decide whether or not we are going to cooperate. Yes, Jeremiah from before he was born was assigned the role of prophet in God's great plan. However, when he got the call, he could have said no. It is the same with each of us. We have been assigned a role; some are destined for greatness, others have a more humble part to play. But whether we eventually conform ourselves to that envisaged destiny is another matter. It is our choice. Such a solution, of course, lays the stress on choice, and waters down the type of determinism normally associated with predestination. Unfortunately, taking into account God's foreknowledge, it seems less than satisfactory. It can strike us as odd that God should have a plan which, through his foreknowledge, he knows is not going to be fulfilled. He will know it to be a waste of time because some of his subjects are simply not going to cooperate.

A better solution might be one where God knows us so well (every hair of our head is numbered, remember) that he can anticipate what choice we would make in any given situation. He then devises an overall plan for the world where everyone's destiny is indeed irrevocably set out, but a world where everyone is at all times doing exactly what they would freely choose to do. Jeremiah, for example, was destined by God to be a great prophet because God knew – before Jeremiah himself – that he had it in him to fulfil such a role and (after initial misgivings) would willingly agree to do it. Under such a scheme, everyone is at all times doing exactly what they choose to do, their actions being a faithful expression of their true nature. They would not want the "freedom" to act otherwise. But at the same time, these selfsame actions are all part of the fabric of the history of the world as devised by God.

I suppose we would have to reckon such a suggestion to be the religious equivalent to the compatibilist argument forwarded in the free will/determinism problem. It is a case of trying to have our cake and eat it! For what it is worth, it is a stance that I for one somewhat favour. But as with all these tricky questions, you might think differently.

Who do you think provided the more accurate assessment of religion: Freud or Jung?

Is it helpful to regard either religion or atheism as a mental virus?

Do we have free will?

8 MIRACLES

- I think that all the miracles took place in the Bible as they're described.

- Science may prove that miracles cannot happen.

- The person who believes in the miracle stories needs to question the morality of their God. It seems absurd to believe in a God that will only help a few and not the many.

- God is an omnipotent being, so he can obey or disobey the laws of nature as he chooses.

- I think that there are modern-day miracles but just not as described in the Bible – things like the circuit board are miracles for me.

- I do think that miracles still occur today, for example, if someone's cured after they've been diagnosed with a terminal illness and there really isn't any other explanation then that must be the result of divine intervention.

- I don't think there is a God who causes miracles. Miracles arise out of superstition, mass hysteria, and like a natural human instinct to want to contemplate the existence of something more.

– Back in the days when religion came about
  and there was miracles… how do you know it
  wasn't just magic or a form of illusion to fool
  people, to say "Yes, come join us!"?

First we need to be clear what we mean by a "miracle". Strictly
speaking a miracle is an event – *any* event – that might be
interpreted as God revealing himself in a special way. There's
a car crash. The survivors have a "miracle escape". They might
thank God for his protection. Events like that don't necessarily
mean a law of nature has been broken. It is all a matter of
what significance you might read into it. No, the problem lies
with those miracles that *would* require a law of nature to be
broken – those recorded in the Bible and the sacred writings
of other religions, together with the miracles claimed to be
happening in our own time. Contemporary miracle accounts
tend to concentrate on acts of healing, with the contentious ones
being those that involve a recovery from a condition that was
previously diagnosed as being incurable or terminal. We think,
for example, of the reported experiences of pilgrims to locations
such as Lourdes in France.

Such claims are always hard to assess. Was the original condition
misdiagnosed? It is well known that even without calls for God's
aid, the human body has remarkable powers of self-healing. This
ability, of course, might in itself be claimed to be a "miracle",
but only in the looser sense of a natural phenomenon that can
be interpreted by the faithful as God revealing his concern for
human welfare. In other words, God has incorporated into the
very fabric of the created world an answer to prayer without
there being any need for the smooth running of the laws of
nature to be interrupted.

But back to what we might call "proper" miracles. One
approach is simply to deny that they happen; belief in them is
due to wishful thinking and gullibility. The Scottish philosopher,

David Hume, famously declared:

No testimony is sufficient to establish a miracle unless the
testimony be of such a kind, that its falsehood would be more
miraculous than the fact which it endeavours to establish.
(An Enquiry Concerning Human Understanding)

This, in our scientific age, has become a widely accepted view.
Many people, including those who count themselves religious, go
along with it. Some would go as far as to claim that modern-day
science has *proved* that miracles cannot happen. But is that the
case? Science certainly demonstrates that the laws of nature are
obeyed with remarkable consistency, to the extent that we are
today understandably more cautious of accepting miracle claims
than people of former times. But that in itself is no proof that
there might be exceptions to the general rule. The Viennese-
born British philosopher Karl Popper was at pains to point out
that, strictly speaking, the laws of nature are never verified. It
had previously been claimed that the very definition of what
constituted a scientific statement was that it could be verified.
This was the so-called *verification principle*. Popper, on the
other hand, argued that what actually singled out a statement
as being scientific was that it was open to being falsified – that
there was a possibility of some future counter-evidence coming
forward that showed that the statement was *not* true, or at least
not in all circumstances. Indeed, the history of science is littered
with examples of laws that were generally thought to have been
verified beyond all doubt, only for it to be realized later that they
were at best but approximations to the truth. Such revelations
come when the investigation of those laws is extended to cover
more extreme situations than normal.

For instance, there is Newton's inverse square law of gravity.
With the advent of Einstein's general theory of relativity, it came
to be recognized that Newton's law completely breaks down under

conditions of very strong gravity, such as we get close to a black hole. For more normal conditions, for instance when working out the motion of planets about the Sun, Newton's law is a very good approximation (and much simpler to handle!), so it is still used. But we now know that it cannot handle all situations.

Then again we have the well established law of conservation of energy. Energy can take on different forms, but the total amount remains the same. Except that it doesn't – not under all circumstances. Under extreme conditions – this time when dealing with very small entities such as subatomic particles – there can be energy fluctuations. These are manifestations of the quantum uncertainty we came across earlier.

As one further example, imagine two cars approaching each other from opposite directions, one travelling at 30 m.p.h. and the other at 40 m.p.h. What is their relative approach speed? It is obvious; we have simply to add the two speeds: $30 + 40 = 70$ m.p.h. And that, indeed, is what a pedestrian at the side of the road finds to be the case. But according to relativity theory, for the drivers themselves their approach speed is slightly less than 70 m.p.h. Not by very much; the difference is hardly detectable. That is why we are happy to carry on thinking that it is 70 m.p.h. for all observers. But if in our mind's eye the vehicles were travelling close to the speed of light, denoted by c, whereas the pedestrian would claim the approach speed was $2c$, the drivers would say it was c. In other words, our familiar, seemingly commonsense, procedure for combining speeds in a case like this (i.e. just add them together) does not work when dealing with unusual conditions – this time when dealing with extreme speeds.

In summary, what we find from these examples is that our familiar laws of physics – those conventionally taught in schools – are perfectly adequate for dealing with normal everyday life, but can break down under exceptional conditions such as strong gravity, small size, high speed. It was for this reason that Popper spoke out against the verification principle for defining what constituted a scientific statement. He instead substituted his *falsification principle*.

Bearing this in mind, we might conclude that although it is perfectly reasonable in the light of modern science to adopt a somewhat sceptical attitude towards miracle claims, it is going too far to hold that science has proved or ever will prove the impossibility of there being the occasional exception to the rule.

What sort of exceptions? Christians hold that Jesus was the Son of God in human form. There had never previously been such a situation, nor has there been one since. It was a one-off set of circumstances. That might have been reason enough for unusual things to happen. And if miracles might have happened then, why not at other times when, for whatever reason, circumstances might have been regarded by God as exceptional?

This assumes, of course, that God is *capable* of violating the laws, should he so wish. For the religious believer this is not a problem. Why are there laws in the first place? God set them up. Being the author of the laws, he presumably has no difficulty setting them aside on occasion if he so chooses to do. It becomes not a question of whether God can so act, but whether he *chooses* to interrupt the otherwise smooth running of his world in this way.

In order to gain insight into whether God does so choose, and if so under what circumstances, we look to Jesus and his approach to miracles. We read that during his temptations in the wilderness it was suggested to him that he throw himself off a high building. Such an act would, of course, have been a sure-fire way of getting the attention of the people and demonstrating who he was. But he set his face against such a gratuitous use of his divine power. Later in his ministry, when he was taunted by the Pharisees to prove his credentials by some miraculous display, he replied, "A wicked and adulterous generation asks for a miraculous sign!" (Matthew 12:39). The story of the rich man and the poor beggar

Lazarus has the former in hell, while Lazarus is with Abraham in heaven. The rich man implores Abraham to send Lazarus to his five brothers so that they will be converted and thus spared the torment that he himself was enduring. Abraham refuses, saying, "If they do not listen to Moses and the Prophets, they will not be convinced even if someone rises from the dead" (Luke 16:31). At Jesus' crucifixion, he refused to end his suffering by coming down from the cross in response to the jibes hurled at him.

From all this, we can conclude that Jesus was against the unjustified use of miraculous power. It was not to be used in an attempt to convert people. And we can understand why. It is held that the supreme characteristic of God is love, and that we are to enter into a loving relationship with God, and with each other. Love is not something that can be forced. It has to be freely offered from the heart. Spectacular displays of miraculous power could not have done otherwise than to coerce people into conforming to God's will. Most of the miracles in the Bible are not of that sort. Time and again we are informed, either by word or by action, that the people witnessing and benefiting from Jesus' miracles were already faithful believers. They did not need demonstrations of this kind in order to be won over. For them, faith had come first and, only later, the experience of the miracle; it was not the other way round. There are a few apparent exceptions to this rule. We think, for example, of Paul being struck down, blinded, and hearing Jesus' voice from heaven on his way to Damascus to persecute Christians there. On the surface, this seems to be a case of someone being forced into a belief against their very nature. But we must not be hasty. Who is to tell what previous misgivings Paul might have been having about what he had been doing? Perhaps he had been agonizing over it for some time, only for it all to come to a head on that occasion. At last he had come face to face with the abject realization that he had been wrong all along, and needed to undergo a radical change, regardless of the likely consequences – his eventual execution for the cause.

We cannot, of course, be sure what was going on in his mind at the time. We are simply pointing out that there might be more to Paul's conversion than is apparent at first.

Bearing all this in mind, can the religious believer now happily go ahead and accept, lock, stock, and barrel, all the miracles recorded in the Bible or in other sacred Scriptures?

Perhaps not. The first question to be asked of any miracle account is whether there might be some perfectly natural explanation of the phenomenon. It has been suggested, for example, that the parting of the Red Sea, to allow the Israelites to escape from Egypt, might have been due to freak weather conditions: a very high wind forcing the water to retreat. The feeding of the Israelites in the desert on manna and quails almost certainly has an easy explanation. Manna is a syrupy secretion given out by insects, *Trabutina mannipara*, on the leaves of tamarisk plants between May and July. It then falls to the ground as drops the size of peas, and Bedouin Arabs gather them in the morning. Flocks of quails migrate from Africa across Palestine in the spring. Some do not make it, and fall to the ground exhausted. The casting out of devils by Jesus might today be regarded as the work of a good psychiatrist. It has been suggested that a possible explanation of the feeding of the five thousand is that many in the crowd had brought food with them. It was intended for themselves. But when a few loaves and fishes were initially offered, that gesture led the others also to share what they had brought.

The next question to ask of a miracle account is whether the story might have been generated by a misunderstanding of some sort. Take, for example, the story of Jesus walking on water. The disciples are in a boat on Lake Galilee. They see Jesus walking on the water. Impetuous Peter gets out of the boat in an attempt to do the same, but ends up floundering. It is a curious story. Why should Jesus, having previously rejected the idea of defying gravity by throwing himself off a high building, choose to defy gravity by walking on water – and for no particularly useful purpose? The story is similar to another in which, soon after Jesus' resurrection, the disciples are once again in a boat on Lake Galilee. They see Jesus on the seashore. Peter again gets out of the boat, this time to swim to Jesus. The main difference in the stories is that in one of them Jesus is on the sea, and in the other he is on the seashore. In this connection, biblical scholars have pointed out that in the original version of the miracle story, the Greek phrase *epi tes thalasses* can be translated as either "on the sea" or "by the sea". It has therefore been argued that these accounts refer to one and the same incident, Jesus being by the sea (i.e. on the seashore), and that somewhere along the line, in the telling and retelling of the story, someone has got hold of the wrong end of the stick and inadvertently created a miracle story. This view gains added support from the fact that when the disciples allegedly saw Jesus walking on the water, they declared, "It's a ghost." This might well have been a very understandable reaction on seeing Jesus on the seashore after his resurrection.

But having said all this, very few of the miracle stories can be accounted for in these ways. So what about the others?

It is here religious believers have to come to terms with an uncomfortable fact: people in ancient times did not think scientifically, the way we do today. Far from it. They took a positive delight in tales of wondrous happenings. We see a little of that going on even in our own times with tales of alien abductions and the mysterious formation of crop circles. But in earlier days this cavalier tendency was far more pronounced. We see it in the many apocryphal writings that failed to get into the Bible ("apocryphal" meaning "questionable"). These include *The Gospel of Peter*, *The Infancy Gospel of Thomas,* and *The Arabic Gospel of the Childhood.* Here we read, for example, of how a man had been turned into a mule. Mary placed the infant Jesus on his back, and the mule turned back into the man. Jesus as a schoolboy made a bird out of clay, which promptly came to life and flew out of the window. One day a boy accidentally ran into Jesus; Jesus cursed him and he immediately fell down dead. Peter converted many people by throwing a kipper into the water, and it came back to life. A magician, in dispute with Peter, levitated himself to a great height above the city. The crowd were most impressed. Peter called upon God, whereupon the magician's power was switched off, he fell to earth, breaking his leg in three places. The story ends happily with the crowd stoning the fellow to death and declaring that they were now Christians!

Such tales, of course, strike us as being absolutely absurd. Apart from their improbability, they are so out of keeping with the nature of Jesus and what his mission was all about. It is no wonder they were excluded from the Bible. Nevertheless, the prevalence of such writings outside of the Bible does inevitably raise a worry that the same kind of thing – to a much lesser extent, one hopes – might be going on *within* the Bible.

This concern gains weight when we consider the manner in which we come to have our present day Bible. It was not until AD 90 that the contents of the Old Testament were decided. Even then there remained a dispute between the Palestinian Jews and the Hellenistic Jews, the latter insisting on including extra writings, known today as the Old Testament Apocrypha. As for the New Testament, it was not until the second century that the idea arose of having an additional testament to cover the life and teaching of Jesus and of the early disciples. Early in the fourth century we have Bishop Eusebius compiling a list whereby the candidate writings were assigned to one of three categories: "acknowledged", "disputed", and "spurious". By AD 340 the list had become the same as our present New Testament, with the exception of the book of Revelation, which did not make it onto the list until the end of the fourth century, at which point the list was closed. Even so, it was recognized that some of the writings excluded doubtless contained genuine teachings of Jesus. *The Gospel of Peter*, for instance, continued to be widely used long after. But, on balance, it lost out. By a similar token, we suspect that some of the writings that successfully got into the Bible did so because, on balance, their good features outweighed the less helpful aspects.

From this chequered history, we see that the early church had no clear unambiguous way of deciding what constituted Scripture. Accordingly, we too ought to exercise caution when assessing, in particular, the miracle accounts.

We begin by placing the books of the New Testament in chronological order – the order in which they were written, rather than that in which we find them today. First we have the epistles of Paul. Then comes the first of the Gospels, which was that of Mark. Next we have the Gospels of Matthew and Luke, both of whom used Mark as one of their sources. Finally we have John's Gospel.

What we find is that Paul's letters, the earliest of the writings, contain no reference to any miracles, apart from the resurrection of Jesus. None at all. The first of the Gospels, Mark, includes the resurrection, but also accounts of miracles. Matthew and Luke include Mark's miracle stories, but additional ones as well. Finally, John's Gospel includes even more miracles. Thus, as biblical scholars point out, we gain the impression that perhaps the number of miracle stories in circulation was increasing with time.

This suspicion is heightened on examining one or two particular stories in detail. Take, for instance, Jesus calling the fishermen Simon, Andrew, and James to become his disciples. In Mark's account, Jesus simply tells them to follow him. They immediately agree to do so. The same thing happens in Luke, but only after they have had a miraculous haul of fish – one so great as to cause Peter to fall on his knees before Jesus and for his companions also to be completely overcome. We cannot help but wonder why Mark did not mention this miraculous occurrence.

Then we have the account of the arrest of Jesus in the Garden of Gethsemane the night he was betrayed by Judas. Mark describes how one of Jesus' followers cut off the ear of the servant of the high priest. And that was that. But in Luke's Gospel Jesus miraculously restores the ear – an astonishing act of healing. But if this actually happened, why no word about it from Mark? We can understand why a miracle account might appear in one Gospel and not in another; one of the writers was not aware of the incident. But here we have the writers describing the *same* incident. Why would Mark omit the all-important punchline? Could it be that at the time Mark was writing, there was no punchline?

Questioning the miracle accounts is a serious matter for Christians. Christianity is fundamentally a historical religion. It crucially depends on certain historical facts: that there was a man Jesus; he was a teacher; he was crucified, died, and was buried; he rose from the dead. As Paul says, "If Christ be not risen, then is our preaching vain, and your faith is also vain" (1 Corinthians 15:14). In view of this, many believers are extremely wary of calling into question the historical accuracy of any part of the Bible. They are fearful that this might be the beginning of a very slippery slope. Where will it all end?

At the very outset, when we were considering the Genesis account of Adam and Eve, we noted that the Bible is a collection of different kinds of writing. Yes, there are historical accounts, but also myths, songs, proverbs, and so on. And the individual books do not necessarily lend themselves to easy categorization. It is unwise to regard a book as being, for example, pure history – completely unaffected by other types of writing that were going on at the same time. John's Gospel, for instance, is to be regarded as history strongly influenced by an interpretation of the broader context, meaning, and significance of what is being described.

So it is that when we come to consider the miracle accounts, we have to be open to the possibility that we might not, in all cases, be dealing with a straight recitation of historical facts. There might be something else going on; we might be missing a subtler point. What might that be? Well, one of the things that distinguishes the miracle accounts in the Bible from those in the writings excluded from the canon is that most of them appear to have some deep spiritual connection.

When, for example, Jesus feeds the five thousand, he refers to himself as the Bread of Life. Anyone who comes to him will never hunger. He is pointing to a different kind of hunger – a hunger for meaning in life. His provision of the physical food is to be seen as an analogy for his ability also to provide spiritual nourishment. Again, at the healing of the man born blind, Jesus makes mention of the spiritual blindness of the Pharisees who are looking on at the time, and he speaks of himself as the Light of the World. At the raising of Lazarus from the dead, Jesus declares, "I am the resurrection and the life. Those who believe in me will live, even though they die; and whoever lives and believes in me will never die" (John 11:25–26). The point is being made that eternal life is not something we have to wait for. We are embarked upon it already in the midst of this mortal life. The miraculous haul of fish we noted just now is an analogy for what really is important in that story, namely that the fishermen were to become "fishers of men". The healing of the ear of the high priest's servant is accompanied by Jesus' command to put down the sword because all who live by the sword, die by it.

What of the virgin birth – the account of Jesus being born of the woman Mary, but being conceived by the Holy Spirit? We cannot imagine a more vivid way of getting across the conviction that Jesus was a unique blend of the human and the Divine. Whether, in addition, we have to regard it as a statement of historical fact might be seen as another matter. It seems peculiar, for instance, that Paul in his writings, when trying to get across the uniqueness of Jesus as the Son of God, did not refer to the virgin birth as clear confirmation of his teaching. Presumably, at the time of his writing, he had not heard of it. Was that because the story only came into circulation sometime later, when Jesus' followers were wrestling with the problem of how to convey to others just how different Jesus was from all previous prophets and holy men?

The turning of water into wine, as recorded in John's Gospel, makes for an interesting case study. It illustrates just how complex and sophisticated a biblical miracle story can be. The scene is a wedding reception. The wine is running out. An embarrassment for the host certainly, but one might think hardly a situation warranting the performance of a miracle. Moreover, we learn that the guests were already "well drunk". When Mary draws Jesus' attention to the shortage, clearly expecting him to do something about it, Jesus replies, "Dear woman, why do you involve me? My time has not yet come" (John 2:4). It appears to be a straight rejection. But then, we are told, he nevertheless goes ahead with a miracle, which seems odd – out of character.

On looking into the matter in greater depth, we first note that transformations involving wine have a special significance for Christians. In the Holy Communion service, lowly wine is said to be transformed in some sense into the blood of Christ. So are we to assume that at the wedding feast at Cana, through the transformation of lowly water into wine, an allusion is being made to that other kind of transformation? This is confirmed when we note that, when referring to the servants who bring the pots of water to Jesus, John does not use the usual term for a servant. He uses the word meaning deacon – the person who, in a traditional Holy Communion service, brings the wine to the priest to be transformed. The next point to note is that Jesus does not create a little extra wine sufficient only to cover the deficiency, but 120 to 180 gallons of it – a gesture indicative of the overflowing abundance of God's response to prayer. Then we further note that the original purpose of the water was that it was intended "for purification" – the ceremonial washing of hands before the meal. But to the Jewish mind, one is cleansed, in a spiritual sense, through the Law of Moses. Jesus in his ministry was to declare that he had not come to set aside the Law but to fulfil it. The bringing of the water to Jesus can therefore be seen as symbolic of the bringing of the Law to him to have it fulfilled. The setting of the miracle is a wedding. On another occasion, Jesus refers to himself as the bridegroom. When asked why his disciples did not fast, he replied that while the bridegroom was with them, that was not a time to mourn. Eventually, when the bridegroom was taken away, then they would fast. Did Jesus have this in mind when he said to his mother, "My hour has not yet come"? That is to say, the hour when he would be taken away (to be crucified) had not yet come, so this was indeed a time for rejoicing. In other words, far from rejecting Mary's request, which we have been assuming was the case, Jesus was in fact agreeing to do something about it. Finally we note the opening words of the story: "On the third day…" Ostensibly it refers to the third day after a conversation Jesus had had with Nathanael. But, as is well known, the story of Jesus' resurrection begins with the same words – this time referring to the third day after the crucifixion. That being the case, we suspect that Jesus' followers would automatically see a link between the rejoicing of the wedding feast and the rejoicing that accompanied Jesus' resurrection.

Thus we find that what on the surface seems to be a simple account of a magical trick – the turning of water into wine – can be read as a deeply meaningful reflection, full of subtle allusions to a number of spiritual themes. Which still leaves open the question as to whether it is more than just an allegory. In addition to all the symbolism, did the event actually, physically occur? John concludes his account by recording that this was indeed the first of Jesus' miracles, and that it revealed his glory to the disciples. This appears to indicate that John did expect his readers to accept it as a literal account of what happened, as well as appreciating its significance.

This becomes for us a recurring problem affecting most of the miracle accounts. Having noted their spiritual undertones – the underlying messages relevant to how we should be living our own lives – do we in addition accept them as historical events? What has been said so far doubtless inclines one to be cautious, not to say sceptical. But there is a further factor we need to take into account – one that operates in the opposite sense.

When faced with someone in trouble or distress, we know what we would do. We would do all in our power to help such a person (or at least I hope we would). It is the only kind, compassionate, loving thing to do. Jesus during his ministry was often faced with just such situations. People would come to him with all manner of illnesses and disabilities, wanting him to cure them. If Jesus was indeed the Son of God, then it would have been in his power so to act. Jesus being the perfect personification of God's supreme love for humanity would surely be bound to do all in *his* power to help. And if that were to include the ability to bring about a miraculous recovery, then surely the demands made of him to be perfect in love would have compelled him so to act. He could hardly have refrained from helping. Thus we can well imagine that in these situations Jesus would have felt himself more or less forced to perform a miracle. These were not acts aimed at converting people. As we noted, in almost all the cases the person benefiting from the miracle had already expressed their confidence in him. Also we note that Jesus is sometimes reported as telling witnesses to the miracle not to tell anyone about it. It is almost as though he was embarrassed at being put in this position of having to wield his divine power. He did not want his loving compassionate act to be further used to coerce other people into a belief in him. This line of reasoning, therefore, might incline us to be more sympathetic to the acceptance of miracles of healing, and perhaps others where there might also be a loving motive at work.

Finally we need to address one particular miracle that stands out as having exceptional importance for Christians: Jesus' resurrection. As we earlier noted, Paul declared that if Christ is not risen from the dead, then the Christian faith is in vain. There are many facets we need to consider. In the first place, we need to recognize that the idea of someone coming back to life again sounded as unlikely to the ancient Jews as it does to us today. The disciple Thomas was not the only one to be sceptical until provided with concrete proof – the ability to actually touch the living Christ again. It has been suggested that the disciples stole the body and made up the story of him coming back to life. But to what purpose? No one was going to believe such a silly tale. Was it to prove to the Jews that Jesus had indeed been their long awaited Messiah? No. There had been no expectation of the Messiah coming back from the dead. Furthermore, making up such a story would have robbed the Christians of a powerful rallying call: the indignation and anger welling up from the unfair, shameful, wicked death of their innocent leader. The blood of martyrs has often been the spur to powerful movements and rebellions. But the disciples were not indignant; they did not cry for revenge or justice; they did not scatter in defeat. Instead, they were overwhelmed by a sense of joy and of victory. Having initially been a frightened band huddling behind locked doors for fear of their enemies, they emerged transformed and only too willing to lay down their lives for a cause that they were now convinced had been victorious. Can we seriously think that this change would have been brought about as a result of a clandestine meeting where the disciples had got together to cook up an absurd story of Jesus coming back to life – a story they knew to be utterly false? It is not as though the disciples, having left their homes and families and followed the teaching and example of Jesus for the past few years, were the sort of people likely to suddenly change into a bunch of pathological liars. The most powerful evidence in favour of the truth of the resurrection account lies in the transformation of the disciples. It appears likely that something quite extraordinary must have happened to bring this about.

However, the niggling worry we are bound to have concerning the account is that it came about at a time when, as we have seen, people appeared to have been rather free and easy about claiming miracles. But here we have to note that the account of the resurrection was like no other miracle claim. Jewish miracle accounts were written almost exclusively to a well-established formula. The account was in three parts. First we have the events leading up to the miracle. These are given in sufficient detail to establish that what was to happen really was a miracle. So, for example, we are told that the man was born blind; this was not some passing temporary blindness that might have worn off in the normal course of events; it was a permanent condition. Lazarus was truly dead before he was raised, to the extent that his body stank. In the second part of the story, we have the description of the miracle itself, complete with the words spoken at the time, and often with accompanying actions – for example, the placing of mud on the blind man's eyes. Finally comes the coda. The man could see for the first time. A lame man picked up his bed and walked. The people were astonished. The cured person was overjoyed. This third part is intended to make clear that the occurrence was truly amazing.

But what do we find when we examine the account of the resurrection? The first part of the story is there: all the events leading up to Jesus' arrest, his trial, flogging, his crucifixion, the dividing of his garments, the spear being thrust into his side. He was clearly dead. The third part of the story is also there: his appearances to the women followers and to the disciples, including doubting Thomas; his eating with them; what he said to them; his ascension. All this unequivocally establishes that something extraordinary had indeed happened. But what of the second part of the story – the all-important description of the miracle itself – Jesus getting up from the stone slab on which his body had been laid and emerging from the tomb? It is not there. The crucial part of the story is entirely missing. No one brought up in the Jewish culture of the time would have dreamt of creating a miracle story like that. The testimony has come down to us in this form presumably because that is what actually happened. It is the imperfect, incomplete account of a historical event.

We can see how offensive the account sounded to Jewish ears in the way that gradually over time descriptions of the event came to be modified in an attempt to fill in the gap. The earliest Gospel writer, Mark, describes how there was a man in a white robe by the empty tomb. In the later Gospel according to Matthew, the man has become an angel (an interpretation perhaps helped by the fact that during the first century angels were not thought of as having wings). By the time we get to Luke and John, the angel is joined by a second angel. Whereas in Mark the stone has already been rolled aside, the later Matthew has a half-hearted attempt at filling in the gap by having the women witness the angel coming down from heaven and rolling the stone away from the mouth of the tomb to the accompaniment of an earthquake.

But it is not until we come to the apocryphal writing of *The Gospel of Peter* that we find a really good account of the actual miracle. Two men encircled with light descend and roll the stone away. The onlookers see

> … *three men coming out of the tomb, the two supporting the one, and a cross following them, and the heads of the two reached as far as heaven, but that of Him that was led overtopped the heavens. And they heard a voice from heaven saying, "Hast thou preached to them that sleep?" And a response was heard from the cross "Yea".*

And so it goes on. Miracle story writing at its most imaginative!

But nothing like what we find in the first accounts of that first Easter morning.

Next we note that the Bible records what are supposed to be eyewitness accounts. The police reliably inform us that genuine eyewitness accounts have distinguishing characteristics that are absent from fabrications. In the first place, there are inconsequential details mixed up with the important facts we need to know. We find ourselves thinking, "Please get to the point." Accordingly, we find in John's Gospel how two disciples run to the tomb. One gets there first, but for some unknown reason does not immediately go in. He waits and lets the other go in first. Why bother to tell us this? It is of no importance. It is there in the account because that is presumably what happened.

Then we note that unexpected scenes are remembered by an eyewitness with especial vividness. It is as though the scene they are recalling is still etched in the mind's eye. As they describe it, it is almost as though they are talking about something they can still see in all its detail. Accordingly, we find that when the disciples go into the tomb they are astonished to find that it really is empty. There are the clothes on the slab. The cloth that was round Jesus' head is lying a little apart from the other clothing. Again it is something of no significance. It is mentioned solely because that is what they happened to see.

Sometimes an eyewitness, embarrassingly, is not able to account for his or her own actions. Just imagine how shamefaced the two followers felt on telling the disciples that they had met the risen Jesus on the road to Emmaus, invited him into their home, and sat down to a meal with him before they even recognized who he was! How could they not have recognized him? They simply didn't know. It was not until he broke the bread that "their eyes were opened". Was it something about the way he broke the bread that brought them to their senses? Was this something to do with what they had heard from the disciples about the breaking of bread at the last supper? Who knows? Again, it just reads as an honest account of something that happened. Mary Magdalene had a similar experience. Outside the empty tomb she mistook the risen Jesus for the gardener. It was not until he spoke her name that she recognized him. Here we have to remember that Mary had been a prostitute. Effectively she had been regarded as just a body to give pleasure. It must have meant so much to her for Jesus to have treated her with respect and called her by name. She would never have forgotten the way he had first said her name. Perhaps that is how Jesus knew that pronouncing her name like that was something special and would help her to recognize him again.

Finally, we note that when comparing true eyewitness accounts with each other, although you would expect them to agree on the main points, there are likely to be minor differences over details. It is when each of the witnesses comes out with exactly the same story that we begin to suspect that they have previously got together to ensure they are all singing from the same hymn sheet. Thus we find that there is confusion in the Gospel accounts as to where exactly Jesus revealed himself after his resurrection. As we pointed out earlier, the Gospel writers do not agree as to whether these occurred in Galilee or Jerusalem. One would have thought that if the early Christians had been involved in some sort of conspiracy, they would have at least gone to the trouble to get their story consistent.

Then there appears to be some confusion over what kind of body Jesus had after his resurrection. In some incidents, it seems non-material in that it can suddenly appear in a locked room; in others, it appears to be material in that Jesus eats food in the normal way. Was it a body that could be touched? Jesus invites Thomas to thrust his hand into his side and put his fingers in the nail holes in his hands. But in his encounter with Mary Magdalene in the garden, he tells her not to touch him because he is not yet ascended to his Father. It appears to be a prohibition against touching him. However, a different translation has Jesus saying that she should stop clinging to him. Perhaps he meant that there would be plenty of opportunity in heaven for loving embraces, but for the time being he needed her to go and tell the disciples what had happened.

In summary, we conclude that there are several reasons for believing that the resurrection accounts ought not to be lumped in with the accounts of other miracles. They are quite different, and need to be considered in a different way from how we might be inclined to view the others. In making up our own mind on the issue, we further need to take into account the fact that Jesus made several references to his forthcoming death and resurrection, and made many assertions about the life that was to come. In addition, there are those Christians today for whom Jesus is a real living presence.

According to our scientific outlook, are miracles possible?

Do they actually happen, or are they just superstitious fairy tales?

Are they stories illustrating spiritual truths?

9 THE RELATIONSHIPS BETWEEN SCIENCE AND BELIEF

- I don't think religions necessarily try and hinder scientific development, but let's just say they don't exactly… help.

- Science is willing to change its views based on observations; faith requires you to ignore these observations to preserve tradition.

- Believers are constantly being forced to rethink their position as science keeps making new discoveries… and catching them out.

- I think that science and religion answer the same questions but they come at it from slightly different angles.

- There is absolutely no conflict between science and religion because they deal with different questions. Religion deals with "why", science deals with "how".

- Although science does provide us with facts, it doesn't necessarily improve life. I think that it's spiritual thought that enhances the mind.

– Religion you have in one hand... and then you have science in the other hand. They're two far-apart worlds but they have something to offer each other.

– Science looks at the facts from an objective viewpoint, whereas religion will often try to impose certain moral and ethical principles upon the type of fact being studied.

– A lot of people make science their religion.

Having in previous chapters seen how science and religious belief impact on each other over specific issues, we end by trying to take an overview as to how we might see these two great enterprises in relation to each other in a general sense.

For many people mention of the two words "science" and "religion" in the same breath brings to mind a third word: "conflict". The Galileo scandal is often cited as typical of the supposed antagonism: religion, hidebound by tradition, fighting a stubborn rearguard action against the inevitable advance of enlightened science. We have seen that, regrettable though that incident undoubtedly was, it was not so much a clash of ideologies as one of personalities: those of Galileo and the Pope.

And yet there are issues even today where there is undoubted conflict between science and at least certain forms of religious belief. We think especially of fundamentalist creationists who reject the theory of evolution, favouring instead a literal interpretation of the Adam and Eve story in Genesis. This is a dichotomy particularly prevalent in the USA. Such people are motivated by a sincerely held respect for Scripture, which in itself is admirable. There is no doubt in my mind that many of them have a deep spiritual life and an intense and genuine love of God. That is what really matters. But it comes at a price. In order to defend their position, they must turn their back on the wealth of evidence in favour of evolution. Indeed, some would say that they open themselves up to the accusation of being intellectually dishonest. That in itself might not be important as far as they themselves are concerned; they have found their own route to God. The trouble comes when the impression is given that in order to be religious we *must* accept a literal interpretation of the Adam and Eve story. People like Richard Dawkins too easily slip into a line of argument which presupposes this to be the case. I can well understand Dawkins's indignation at the attempts made by some fundamentalists in the USA to have the Adam and Eve story taught in biology lessons as a rival scientific theory to that of evolution. It is an indignation I would myself share should the same people wish to impose the six-day creation story as a rival to the big bang theory taught in my physics and astronomy lessons. Indeed, is it not inconsistent of fundamentalists to concentrate solely on getting a literal interpretation of Genesis into biology lessons and not physics lessons? One suspects that there is an underlying illogical, emotional element at work here – one prompted by a distaste for the thought of having been descended from the same ancestors as the apes.

Where Dawkins goes too far is when he gives the impression that evolution poses a fundamental problem for all Christians. In this regard, we recall the famous dispute between Samuel Wilberforce, who was Bishop of Oxford at the time, and Thomas Huxley, a strong advocate of Darwin's theory. This was in 1860, a year after the publication of *On the Origin of Species*. In that debate Wilberforce declared: "The principle of natural selection is absolutely incompatible with the word of God." But it would be wrong to think that this was typical of the church's reaction. We would do well to recall that Darwin was, after all, to be accorded later the considerable honour of being buried in Westminster Abbey. In a sermon delivered in 1879, we have the theologian Stuart Headlam saying:

*Thank God that the scientific men have shattered the idol of
an infallible book... It gives grander notions of God to think
of him making the world by his Spirit through the ages than
to think of him making it in a few days.*

And, of course, such thoughts about the Bible can be traced back
as far as St Augustine who, as we saw earlier, had his own ideas
about the gradual evolution of living forms.

A subtler form of potential conflict with science is to be found
in the idea of Intelligent Design. Inasmuch as its adherents are
quite prepared to accept that evolution has, to some limited
extent, taken place, they do not appear to be on a collision
course. But, as we have noted, this is essentially a "God of the
gaps" type of argument, whereby God's direct intervention is
invoked to fill in the gaps in scientific knowledge. As the gaps
are progressively filled by later discoveries, so there remains less
and less need for such supposed interventions. Believers of this
type are thereby placed in the position where they find scientific
progress unwelcome, as it encroaches on what they previously
regarded as the preserve of religion.

Having said all this, many religious believers are happy to fully
accept the findings of evolutionary science. They see it as God's
way of producing us humans. The world he made was not just a
suitable home for life, but carried within its natural functioning
the potential to bring that very life into existence. Life was not
something God had subsequently to inject from outside, so to
speak, as some sort of afterthought.

A further attack on religion was launched from the field
of psychology. As we have seen, Freud gave the impression of
having explained away belief in God as wish-fulfilment and the
projection of attributes of our earthly father onto an imagined
heavenly Father. Whereas we noted how there was undoubtedly
something to be said in favour of the view that our ideas about
God might to some extent be coloured and distorted in this way,

that did not necessarily imply that the whole notion of God was a fiction. Indeed, through the work of Jung, we found it was possible to regard a religious outlook on life as the mark of a mature person rather than that of someone locked into a childhood neurosis.

Turning aside from what we might call the *conflict model*, let us see how else we might view the relationship between science and religion. A commonly held view is that they are independent of each other – the so-called *independence model*. They each deal with their own separate domain of understanding. They address their own set of questions. So, for example, if we wish to know how the world originated, then we look to science, which is able to come up with its answer in terms of the mechanics of the big bang. If, on the other hand, we are asking a question intended to probe the deeper nature of existence itself, then we turn to religion. Indeed, we find some intellectuals choose to define God as that which is responsible for there being something rather than nothing. If we wish to know how the world operates, we look to science with its uncovering of the laws of nature. But if we are asking why there are intelligible laws in the first place, again we look to religion with its conception of a greater Intelligence. If we are asking how life developed, then we look to the evolutionary biologist for an answer. On the other hand, if we want to know what the meaning and purpose of life might be – in other words, *why* we are here rather than *how* we come to be here – we again turn to religion. Crudely speaking, science is concerned with the how-type questions, whereas religion deals with the why-type questions.

A further contrast often made between science and religion is one of methodology: how they set about their respective enterprises. Science is based on experimentation and the constant revising of our theories in the light of new knowledge. It is always advancing, making fresh discoveries. In contrast, religious belief is based on an unchanging tradition. It is mainly devoted to the preservation of established truth. That, baldly stated, is how many see the relationship. And it has to be said that there is an element of justification in such an assessment. Christians do indeed look back to the life and teaching of Christ, and revere him, in a way that scientists do not accept unquestioningly the pronouncements of great scientists of the past such as Sir Isaac Newton. This is because Christ is held to have lived the perfect life; there is no way of improving on that. Newton, on the other hand, could base his theories only on what was known at the time. As we have seen, subsequent investigations under conditions of very high speed and very strong gravity revealed that Newton's laws of motion and of gravity were but approximations to the truth; they have since been overtaken by the more accurate and comprehensive theories advanced later by Einstein. We do not begin a scientific argument by saying "Yes, but Newton said...", whereas it is perfectly legitimate to rest our religious argument on something Christ, or Muhammad, or the Buddha, or Moses said.

And yet we cannot leave it at that. It is simply not true that religion is unchanging. This becomes obvious if the books of the Old Testament are placed in chronological order – in the order in which they were written, rather than how we find them in today's Bible. It then becomes clear that originally Yahweh, the God of the Jews, was thought to be but one god among many. He was jealous of the others and insisted that the Israelites worship him alone. He was a god of war; he fought on behalf of his chosen people. He was a territorial god; he lived on Mount Sinai. He was the tribal god of the Israelites; he cared nothing for the Egyptians (killing off their first-born children), nor for the Canaanites (he helped his people to take over their land). However, with the insights offered by the prophet Elijah, it came to be recognized that Yahweh was not just a fighting god; he could bring rain to water the crops planted in the land of Canaan (there being no need to pray to the local gods, or baals, who were supposedly the experts in such matters). In acknowledging that Yahweh could make the clouds produce rain – and the clouds are to be found spread across the sky everywhere, not just where the Israelites had settled – it came to be recognized that his influence was everywhere. Thus came the idea that there might be just the one God, and that this one God was in charge of everything. Only at this point could the idea develop that Yahweh was the Creator of the world.

Though he was originally thought to be an angry, vengeful God, Hosea came to the understanding that, just as he, Hosea, could forgive his wayward wife, Yahweh could also be merciful. The lowly shepherd, Amos, had the insight that God was not just interested in the influential, rich, and important people in society; he was equally concerned with peasants like himself. Moreover, he saw God as a God of justice. Up to the time of Jeremiah it was thought that in order to worship God you had to go to the Temple in Jerusalem. But the Babylonians invaded, destroyed the Temple, and took the Jewish people into exile. This disaster brought Jeremiah to the realization that worshipping in the Temple was not all that important. What mattered was worshipping God in your heart. Then with the coming of Christ, we have affirmed the realization that the overriding characteristic of God is love.

Thus we see that contrary to the simplistic view of religion being stuck in the past, over the ages there has been as dramatic a change of views over the nature of God as we have more recently experienced in our understanding of the physical world.

Nevertheless, there does seem to be a big difference in the respective ways science and religion set about trying to gain the knowledge upon which their views are based. Scientific experiments are usually conducted in laboratories under controlled conditions where we seek to exclude all extraneous influences other than the specific ones being investigated. Attempts have been made to replicate these procedures in the religious sphere.

For instance, there have been several investigations aimed at trying to show whether or not intercessory prayer is effective. Prayers would be said on behalf of certain hospital patients, and not for others suffering from the same condition – the latter being the "control group". Early results purported to show a positive outcome. A massive experiment, carried out in the late 1990s, aimed to settle the issue once and for all. It involved 1,200 patients about to undergo coronary bypass surgery. They were told that they might be prayed for or they might not. Half of them were indeed prayed for, but not the others (at least not by the special prayer teams set up for this purpose; one could not, of course, stop friends and relatives praying in the normal way, but the effects of this "background noise" (!) should have evened out between the two groups). Neither the patients nor the doctors and nurses attending them knew to which group each patient belonged. There was, in addition, a third group of 600 patients who were informed that they would be prayed for, and were prayed for. This was to investigate any placebo effect of expecting to do better because of the prayers. The result of this exercise was negative; there was no discernible difference in the recovery rates of the various groups. Of course, such a result is open to various interpretations. We might say, for instance, that the heartfelt prayers of loved ones are much more likely to be effective than those of strangers who know little at all about the individual patients they have been assigned to pray for. In other words, the background noise swamped the signal we were trying to measure. In any case, we perhaps ought to note that the Bible does say, "Do not test the Lord your God" (Deuteronomy 6:16). So we cannot complain that we haven't been warned!

Setting aside such spurious pseudoscientific attempts to justify religious belief, we are faced with a variety of ways in which people come to a belief in God. It might be that the writings of Scripture strike us as being authentic. It could be that in prayer we experience a numinous presence. Or such a presence might be felt in a holy building or when meeting a particularly holy, charismatic person. There might be a convincing answer to prayer. Looking back over our life, we might discern a developing pattern and rationale – a sense that we were being guided. These and other ways of approaching God involve faith. It is no good going down on your knees and saying in effect, "OK, God. This is your opportunity. Make the most of it – if you are there. What have you got to say for yourself?" That would get you nowhere. You have to approach prayer *as though* there were a God. And you have to be prepared to persist over a long time if you are not successful right away. It is very much a case of "faith seeking understanding", in the words of the motto of St Anselm.

Many would see such an approach as very different from what we find in science. Surely scientific investigation is wholly objective; it does not start out with any preconceived notions, it does not require an act of faith. That might be the impression we scientists give, but it is not altogether true. Most experiments are done with some hypothesis in mind. It is this tentative theory that guides which particular experiment we are going to carry out – which one of an almost limitless number of possibilities we think might have the best chance of producing an interesting result. For example, from my own experience, I recall how there was a theory that pointed to the possibility of there being a new property of matter. In anticipation that it might actually exist, it was called *charm*. But that is as far as theory could go. It might exist, or it might not. The only way to find out was to do an experiment. Unfortunately, this would be an experiment lasting years, costing millions of pounds, and involving an army of physicists, engineers, and technicians. I and my colleagues, after much deliberation, decided to go for it. At the outset, I was offering odds of five to one against our finding anything. However, that did not mean that I believed we should correspondingly put in only 20 per cent of the effort. No. In order to see a subatomic particle carrying this elusive property (if it existed), we would have to put in a 100 per cent effort. We would have to carry out the experiment exactly *as though* it were there. We did this, trusting in our own integrity that if we found nothing, we would not try to convince ourselves and others that we had found it – in order to try and justify the expenditure of money, time, and effort. In point of fact, we were indeed the first people to make a direct sighting of a particle carrying charm. But that is beside the point. What I am saying is that the approach of doing everything *as though* we were going to get a positive result is how it is in the search for God through prayer. We have to engage in the exercise wholeheartedly, and yet with the conviction that we will not persuade ourselves we are in contact with God if it turns out that we are actually talking to ourselves. In this regard at least, we might see some similarity between the scientific and religious approaches.

But then again we might argue that once a scientific investigation has been concluded there is no doubt about the result. It was an indisputable fact that we had found a particle carrying charm. Everyone was convinced of the evidence. But where in religion is there incontrovertible evidence for the existence of God – something everyone can agree upon? There is none. So is that not in itself a big difference between science and religious belief?

Here we need to be careful. It is certainly true that science does from time to time offer evidence, such as that for the existence of charm, that seemingly allows for only one interpretation. But not always. Take, for example, the big bang. We saw earlier how the expansion of the universe, though consistent with the idea that such motion had resulted from a great explosion, did not convince the enthusiasts for the steady state theory of the universe. Instead, the evidence for the big bang was cumulative. To the expansion of the universe had to be added arguments based on the microwave background radiation, the primordial abundances of the elements making up the freeze-out mix, the changing nature of the universe as one looked back in time by studying galaxies further and further away, and so on. None of these pieces of evidence, considered in isolation, constituted undeniable proof for a big bang. Each of them could be picked off, one at a time, with some alternative ad hoc explanation. It is only when we survey the whole of the evidence and see how a single hypothesis, the big bang, would at a stroke explain them all that we become convinced of its truth. It is not even as though there was some point in time we could pick out and say, "That was the moment when everyone accepted the hypothesis." The arguments against the big bang just gradually petered out and were no longer discussed in scientific circles.

The same could be said of belief in God. There is no single clinching piece of evidence. Instead, we have to view all the evidence together – the indications we have alluded to involving answer to prayer, the sense of the numinous, Scripture, reflections on the sense of purpose as we look back on life, etc. The recognition that these various features of life could all be explained by the single hypothesis that there is a God behind it all is what convinces the religious believer. There need be no sudden "conversion experience". For many, at some indefinite stage in their life, they found they were no longer questioning God's existence.

Having said all that, however, we must not overdo the similarities. There is much to be said in favour of the independence model, both as to the questions science and belief address, and the way they go about finding answers. In certain regards, they do indeed seem to be addressing different kinds of issue, and in their own very different kinds of way.

Which brings us to the next model: the *interaction model*. This is based on the observation that there are times when science and religion appear to be addressing the same rather vague question – "What is it all about?" – but are approaching the subject from different viewpoints, so allowing each to offer its own particular insights. The situation might be likened to the viewing of a 3-D film. Each eye is viewing the same scene, but from a different angle. Each has something useful to contribute. Put the two together to produce a three-dimensional image and we have a much fuller, richer indication as to what is going on. A complete appreciation of the scene is not available to either viewpoint on its own; we need both.

As a further analogy take, for example, the examination of a painting that is alleged to be by Rembrandt. An art expert will view it purely as a work of art, comparing its style, subject matter, the brush strokes, its mood, and so on with other authenticated Rembrandts, and will enquire into its provenance – the evidence of former owners, galleries that might have exhibited it in the past, and indeed whether the work might be traced back to the artist himself. A scientist, on the other hand, has a completely different approach. The paint, the canvas, and the framework will be subjected to chemical analysis to see whether they are consistent with the materials used in the time of Rembrandt. The painting will be X-rayed to see what lies underneath. It might be irradiated by a neutron beam to induce temporary radioactivity – a further method for checking on the paints used and any under-painting not detectable by X-rays. The art connoisseur/historian and the scientist: two quite independent approaches to the same subject. When combined, the hope is that they will lead to an answer to the question of authenticity.

In the field of science and religion, recall how the Adam and Eve story carried the message that we humans are deeply flawed creatures. We might be made in the image of God, and thus have the potential to be like God, but we persistently fall short of that ideal. This is because of an inbuilt tendency to be selfish – taking what does not belong to us – and generally being disobedient to God's will for us. And let's not fool ourselves; the story is talking about you and me – in fact, about everyone, not just a couple of individuals supposedly living a long time ago.

The name "Adam" means "man". This tendency to be self-centred rather than God-centred, as we noted earlier, is known as original sin. This insight into human nature was gathered from the close observation of human behaviour. It incorporates the recognition that babies are not as sweet and innocent as we like to think – as any parent will realize when the youngster does not get exactly what it wants when it wants it! That much has been recognized for at least 3,000 years. Then along comes the theory of evolution by natural selection, with its idea of genetically influenced behaviour patterns. And among those patterns, honed in the evolutionary survival struggles of our ancestors, is to be found an innate tendency, from the moment of conception, to be selfish – putting one's own needs first, even possibly to the point of being aggressive. In this way we have, for the first time, a scientific explanation of a feature that was first addressed through religious thought.

As a second example of theology wrestling with the same sort of problem as is tackled by science, we have the subject of time and its origins. St Augustine, in addition to having his own ideas about an evolutionary type of theory, had worked out long before today's cosmologists that time was as much a feature of the world as any other and would have had to have been created along with everything else. Not having the advantage of knowing about relativity theory's four-dimensional spacetime, he had to use a different line of argument to that of today's cosmologists. But nevertheless he got to a similar conclusion – and 1,600 years before Stephen Hawking!

A particularly interesting example of theologians and scientists tackling the same sort of problem and arriving at similar conclusions is offered by way of quantum theory. This was developed in the twentieth century to account for our observations of the smallest constituents of matter. Its findings about what could and could not be said on the subject appear to have been foreshadowed by theological thought as to what might and might not be said about God. It is instructive to look into this case in some depth.

We begin with what at first sight appears to be a straightforward question: What is an electron? As is well known, the electron is a constituent of matter – part of the make-up of an atom – the atom consisting of a central nucleus surrounded by tiny electrons. Some liken the atom to a miniature Solar System, with the nucleus as the Sun and the electrons as planets. This leads us to think of the electron as being a small particle. And this conclusion is borne out when we examine how electrons interact. In the old-style TV sets built around a cathode ray tube, electrons are fired from a gun at the back of the tube and arrive at the fluorescent screen at the front to produce the picture. Both in the manner in which it is emitted and how it later strikes the screen, the electron behaves like a particle. However, as it passes from the gun to the screen it behaves like a wave – a long drawn-out wave consisting of a succession of humps and troughs. Any experiment designed to investigate how electrons move through space comes up with the same conclusion: one is dealing with a wave.

But how can this be? How can something be both a tiny localized particle and at the same time a spread-out wave? This is the so-called *wave–particle paradox*. And it is not a problem confined to electrons. Light is afflicted in the same way. As light moves through space – passing through lenses, prisms, gaps in barriers – its behaviour is that of waves. Its wavelength (the distance between successive humps) determines the colour of the light, the wavelength of red light being almost twice that of violet light. But on arriving at its destination – the retina at the back of your eye, for instance – it gives up its energy as though it were a tiny bullet-like particle – what we have called a photon. Again we are faced with the wave–particle paradox. The same is even the case when dealing with the nucleus of an atom. A beam of nuclei shows all the characteristics expected of a wave as it moves through space, but instantly appears to revert to a hail of bullet-like particles on arriving at its destination and interacting with other particles.

How were we to explain such strange behaviour? Was the electron *really* a particle, but one that got a bit "wavy" at times? Was light *really* a wave, but one that got a bit "grainy" at times? A radical solution to the problem was offered by the Danish physicist Neils Bohr. He claimed that we simply had to stop asking the question "What is an electron?" or "What is light?" Such questions are meaningless. All we can do is address the question "How does an electron (or light, etc.) behave in a given set of circumstances?" The emphasis is on *observed behaviour*, not on what something *is*. Thus, if the question is to do with how something moves through space between the points A and B, then the answer is in terms of a wave. On the other hand, if the question is to do with how it interacts at point A or B, then the answer is in terms of a particle. The electron or light cannot be passing between A and B and at the same time be *at* A or B, so there is no call to use the words "wave" and "particle" at the same time. It is one or the other. Hence, as far as observed behaviour is concerned, there is no paradox.

Bohr went on to point out that the words "wave" and "particle" – and indeed all the terms we use in science – are specifically designed to account for our observations of the world; they are not meant for describing the world as it is in itself as distinct from its observed behaviour. Any attempt to apply these words to a world that is not being observed amounts to a misuse of language – and results in paradox. In other words, what Bohr was maintaining is this: It was originally thought that the job of science was to describe the world. In order to do this, we have to observe it, i.e. do experiments on it. But having made our observations, what we write down in our physics textbooks is a description of the world as it is, whether or not it is still being observed. However, according to Bohr, what has been written down is not a description of the world at all. Rather it is a description of what it is like to observe the world. His point of view was put forward in the 1920s, and came to be known as the *Copenhagen Interpretation* of quantum physics, so named after the place where Bohr worked.

Not everyone went along with it. Einstein himself was a strong opponent. He made many attempts to demonstrate that it was indeed possible to make meaningful statements about the world divorced from the act of observation, but all proved unsuccessful. Nevertheless, he maintained to his dying day that the ultimate goal of science remained what we always thought it was: the description of the world in itself. Even today the issue continues to be controversial, though it would seem that the Copenhagen Interpretation is the more generally accepted solution to the dilemma posed by the wave–particle paradox.

What has all this to do with science and religion? Simply this: Some eighty years before Bohr wrestled with the problem of what could be said about the nature of the electron and of light, his fellow compatriot, the Danish theologian and philosopher Søren Kierkegaard, was contemplating what might be said about the nature of God. God was the heavenly Father, in other words the Creator of the world. But Jesus was also to be regarded as divine; he was God in human form. Then again we have the Holy Spirit as a further manifestation of God. Thus we have three ways of relating to God: God over us (the Father); God with us (Jesus); and God in us (the Holy Spirit). Thus we get the doctrine of the Trinity: three persons but just the one God. It sounds paradoxical. The mystery is further deepened when we consider the nature of Jesus: fully God, but also fully man. He was not God masquerading as a man, nor a man behaving like God. It is held that he was fully both. But how can that be? God is all-powerful, all-knowing, he is present everywhere at all times; man is not. Again we are faced with a paradox – a paradox with striking similarities to the wave–particle paradox of quantum physics, where it seemed that the electron could be spread out all over the place as a wave, but at the same time be limited to one tiny location as a particle. In 1846, Kierkegaard published his famous work, *Concluding Unscientific Postscript to the Philosophical Fragments*, in which he declared:

> *When subjectivity, inwardness, is the truth, the truth becomes objectively a paradox; and the fact that the truth is objectively a paradox shows in its turn that subjectivity is the truth.*

He was saying that the three-in-one paradox posed by the Trinity and the God/man paradox posed by Jesus were indications that we should cease seeking an answer to the objective question "Who or what is God?" or "Who is Jesus?" and simply rest content with trying to understand how we subjectively *relate* to God and to Jesus. He went on to say:

> *Let us take as an example the knowledge of God. Objectively, reflection (i.e. thought) is directed to the problem of whether this object is the true God; subjectively, reflection is directed to the question whether the individual is related to a something in such a manner that his relationship is in truth a God relationship.*

In effect, the incarnation is telling us of two ways we can relate to Jesus. There are certain situations where it is appropriate to regard Jesus as a human just like us, being subject to the same needs, temptations, and limitations as ourselves. Through Jesus the Godhead truly experiences what it is to be human. But on other occasions it is more appropriate to relate to Jesus as the eternal Son of God, who as such is to be worshipped and adored. Likewise, the Trinity is telling us that there are three ways to relate to God: not only as his Son, but also as our heavenly Father, and as the Holy Spirit. Depending on the particular situation, it is more appropriate to think of God in one or other of these ways. But always we are thinking of a relationship.

Even when thinking of the nature of God himself, the description of the Trinity is in terms of relationships. The Son is begotten of the Father; the Holy Spirit proceeds from the Father and the Son. Admittedly the Nicene Creed goes as far as to say that the Father and the Son are of the same substance (the same Being or essence). And the Athanasian Creed, in stressing that Jesus was both fully God and fully man, says how Jesus is God, of the same essence as the Father, and man, of the same essence of the woman (his mother). Nevertheless, at no time are we defining what this "essence" actually is. All we are saying is that, whatever it is, Jesus has it in common with the Father.

Actually there is nothing new in this. The argument goes back at least as far as the Jewish philosopher Philo (*c*.20 BC – AD 45). He was asking what might be said of the nature of God as he was in himself. His answer was: Nothing. He held that the "essence" of God, as he called it, was absolutely unknowable. Augustine took up the same theme in the fourth century when he said that we could not expect to know the name of the substance of God. The fourteenth-century Eastern Orthodox theologian Gregory Palamas likewise held that we could know nothing of the essence of God. All we could talk meaningfully of are his "energies", that is to say, how God manifests or reveals himself to us in the world. Other theologians, such as Martin Luther, took up the same theme. Nor is this line of thought by any means confined to Christians. It is there in the Jewish tradition, for example, and is especially to the fore in the Baha'i religion.

What is distinctive about Kierkegaard's approach is his emphasis on paradox and the fact that if we encounter paradox, then that can be taken as a warning that we should step back from trying to gain an objective truth and instead be content with a more subjective form of truth. Which is exactly the kind of reasoning that Bohr was to put forward in the twentieth century in connection with his development of the Copenhagen interpretation for dealing with the paradoxes arising out of quantum theory. What I find intriguing is that it is known that Bohr was an avid reader of Kierkegaard. This is not surprising seeing that the latter was born in Copenhagen and also died there. Of Kierkegaard's *Stages on Life's Way,* Bohr once wrote that it was "one of the most delightful things I have ever read". We cannot be sure to what extent Kierkegaard's writings about the paradoxes thrown up by religion might have been the catalyst for the piece of lateral thinking Bohr was to experience when considering the wave–particle paradox. Opinion on this is divided. But it is surely interesting to note that the same type of thinking required for coming to an understanding of God the Creator should also apply to understanding his creation.

These then have been some examples where theologians came to conclusions long before scientists. The interaction can also work the other way. We have seen how the theory of evolution by natural selection, with its description of us humans emerging seamlessly out of the line of other primates, invites theologians to reassess the clear-cut delineation traditionally made between humans and the other animals. A vast difference in terms of intelligence quantitatively, but not a qualitative difference perhaps. The same theory appears also to have something to contribute towards understanding the origins of a moral sense. As we have seen, desirable codes of behaviour can arise in terms of genetically influenced behaviour patterns that are to do with mutual benefit or with sacrifice on behalf of close kin (the selfish gene). But is that the whole story? What of the higher forms of altruism where there does not seem to be any payback? Then we have seen how the possibility thrown up by science that there might be life elsewhere in the universe should encourage theologians to ponder on the significance such a discovery would have, and in particular whether this heralds further incarnations of the eternal Son of God. The suggestion that our universe might be but one universe belonging to a multiverse also has a bearing on the scope and power of God, and how he might go about bringing worlds into existence.

Then there is a subject we have not touched upon at all: the impact of scientific developments and how they affect ethical questions. Among the myriad problems thrown up by medical research, we briefly mention those to do with stem cell research; the question of abortion and when a foetus should be regarded as a living person; the artificial prolongation of life in those patients who without medical assistance would have died, and who wish to be allowed to die; whether there should be some point at which medical treatment and drugs become so prohibitively expensive that they should not be made available; and so on. All such medical breakthroughs act as a challenge to religious people to rethink how they value life.

Such then are various ways in which we might regard religion and science interacting with each other; sometimes one is ahead of the game, sometimes it has been the other way round.

There remains one final model for how science relates to religion, and that is what we might call the *integration model*. About thirty years after the Galileo scandal, the Royal Society was formed in London. It was destined to become the foremost scientific academy in the United Kingdom. It is interesting to note that prominent among its early founding fellows were clergy. Indeed, its first chairman was Bishop John Wilkins.

A later president was to be Sir Isaac Newton, whom many rate as probably the greatest scientist ever. What is not so well known about Newton was that he wrote an estimated 4 million words on theology. He was actually under the impression that he would be remembered more for his contributions to theology than to physics. Then there was that other towering figure of classical physics, James Clerk Maxwell. What Newton did for mechanics and gravity, Maxwell did for electricity and magnetism. Everything electrical in our modern-day life depends for its functioning on the operation of the laws of electromagnetism first formulated by Maxwell. And no one could have been more religiously devout than Maxwell, holding as he did daily family services and Bible readings. Maxwell's theories were, in turn, based on the findings of Michael Faraday, one of the foremost experimental physicists of all time. Faraday too was highly religious; he was a member of the Sandemanian Church, a small Protestant Christian sect founded in 1730 – one that demanded total faith and commitment.

For people such as these, as well as many practising scientists today, it appears only natural that from a study of God the Creator one should go on to study his creation. Our curiosity about God should seamlessly lead to a curiosity about the world. Indeed, there is a branch of theology known as *natural theology*. It seeks to study nature to see what clues it might contain towards a better understanding of God and how God's mind works. According to St Augustine, in coming to understand God we are presented with two "books": the Book of Scripture and the Book of Nature. God reveals himself through the Bible and through religious experience, but also through the physical world. Some have gone as far as to try and *prove* the existence of God by a study of nature. We saw how William Paley, with his example of a watch found on the ground, attempted to do this over the design of the human body. Such claims were doomed and for a time brought natural theology into disrepute. But, providing one is not trying to push the arguments too far, it does appear to many that the study of nature ought to lead to at least some understanding of God – on the assumption that there is indeed a Creator God. After all, when we look at works of art, we often suspect that they betray traits characteristic of the artist who created them. Compare, for example, the tortured works produced by someone like Francis Bacon on the one hand, and on the other, the calm and sublimely peaceful ones of the monk Fra Angelico. We cannot help but conclude that each artist was putting something of themselves into their work. In the same way, we can argue that the study of nature, through science, provides a window into the mind of God.

Thus we have the fourth and final model of how religion and science might relate to each other: the integration model.

So our discussion draws to a close. What do I personally think about the models? Throughout this book, I have tried to keep my own opinions in the background. Not always successfully, I know, but I tried. The aim has been to provide you with the information you need in order to make up your own mind on the issues in a sensible, well-informed manner. As I made clear in the Introduction, I am myself a believer. As such, I fully appreciate that some of my fellow believers might have found some of the things I have said hard to accept. I have in mind those who have problems over evolution, or who found my comments about certain of the miracles hurtful. There was the admission that the avowed atheist, Freud, might well have had something relevant to say about the way we see God. Though the trial of Galileo was not the big science versus religion confrontation, it was nevertheless a shameful episode in church history. And so on. There are those believers who rarely consider such matters. Science impacts very little on their thinking. They have a simple Bible-based faith and prefer for this not to be disturbed. Likewise, there are atheists who are absorbed in science and never give a thought to the wider questions posed by religion. I find both these stances unsatisfactory and unacceptable. As far as I am concerned, the only intellectually honest position is to fully embrace everything that both science and religion are trying to teach us. This in turn means we have to examine how the two domains of understanding relate to each other.

So where do I stand? Which of the four models do I choose? Frankly, I do not see how a clear-cut choice can be made. I see truth in all four. Yes, there can be conflict – particularly as seen from the standpoint of certain kinds of fundamentalist religion, or over ethical challenges. Yes, the two enterprises do at times deal with different types of question, and they go about answering them in their own individual way. Yes, they do interact with each other when addressing the same type of issues, with sometimes the theologians dealing with the questions first before the scientists later come to the same conclusions, and sometimes the scientists get there first, their discoveries throwing up fresh questions for religious people to consider. But my own preference is for the integration model. For me, as it was for the great scientists of the past, it seems only natural that we should progress from a knowledge of the created world to an enquiry into its Creator; from a knowledge of the biology of life, to a quest for the meaning and purpose of life. Similarly, in the reverse direction, awareness of God seems to me to lead in a natural way to a curiosity and appreciation of the world God created.

But, as I have said, what I think is beside the point. What do *you* think?

There are four different ways of viewing the relationships between science and belief:

- **conflict;**

- **independence;**

- **interaction;**

- **integration.**

Which of these alternatives do you prefer?

INDEX